THAT'S ANOTHER CUP OF COFFEE

ONE WOMAN'S INSPIRATIONAL JOURNEY OF COURAGE AND HOPE

By Sara Tenaci

© Copyright 2003 Sara Tenaci. All rights reserved.

No part of this publication may be reproduced, stored in a retrieval system, or transmitted, in any form or by any means, electronic, mechanical, photocopying, recording, or otherwise, without the written prior permission of the author.

Designer
Bob Matthews
Matthews Design Group
Web: matthewsdesigngroup.com
Email: bmatthew@dnai.com

Editor
Jessica Keet
The Proofreaders' Proofreader
Web: www.proofreadersproofreader.com
Email: jessica.proofreader@verizon.net

Printed in Victoria, Canada

```
National Library of Canada Cataloguing in Publication Data

Tenaci, Sara, 1954-
     That's another cup of coffee : one woman's inspira-
tional journey of courage and hope / Sara Tenaci.
ISBN 1-55395-889-6
     I. Title.
F869.C17T45 2003          920.72          C2003-901127-5
```

TRAFFORD

This book was published *on-demand* in cooperation with Trafford Publishing.
On-demand publishing is a unique process and service of making a book available for retail sale to the public taking advantage of on-demand manufacturing and Internet marketing. **On-demand publishing** includes promotions, retail sales, manufacturing, order fulfilment, accounting and collecting royalties on behalf of the author.

Suite 6E, 2333 Government St., Victoria, B.C. V8T 4P4, CANADA
Phone   250-383-6864   Toll-free   1-888-232-4444 (Canada & US)
Fax   250-383-6804   E-mail   sales@trafford.com
Web site   www.trafford.com   TRAFFORD PUBLISHING IS A DIVISION OF TRAFFORD HOLDINGS LTD.
Trafford Catalogue #03-0252   www.trafford.com/robots/03-0252.html

10   9   8   7   6   5   4   3

<u>SARA TENACI</u>
THAT'S ANOTHER CUP OF COFFEE

DEDICATION

Even though my life's journey thus far has been an arduous one, I still believe that I have been blessed. One might ask how I could feel blessed after all I have had to endure? I would be deceiving you if I were to say that belief alone has helped me through this, and that I never had any doubts about God's plan for me. God has blessed me with courage and a tenacious spirit.

Oftentimes I wonder myself where my strength comes from. But when you believe, the answer is clear. When I look in the mirror, it's like looking through a kaleidoscope. It's there, all of it. All the colorful bits and pieces of my life filled with unconditional love from all my family and friends, and it is in them that I find the strength to carry on, and a reason to be the tenacious one.

Millie, Madeline, and Madison, my three beautiful daughters. You are the fire that makes my life glow. With you, my glass is always full. Your unconditional love, unselfishness, and ability to see life through a child's eyes, even as adults, has truly been a blessing for me. My heart overflows with the love and beauty you embrace me with everyday, and I love you.

My husband, **Michael**. What can I say? With every mountain we have had to climb, every blemished road we have had to travel, that seemed to have no end, you are still here with me, and our three wonderful daughters. Without you, I wouldn't have been blessed with Millie, Madeline, and Madison. And...for that, a gift that no one else could ever give me, I will always love you.

Mom and Dad for the unconditional love you fill my life with on a daily basis. For allowing me to be who I am, and for being grandparents to my children in a capacity that can be measured by nothing other than that of pure love.

Tony, my baby brother, I love you. You are always there for me, and I will always be there for you. You too, have given me a blessing, your five beautiful daughters, whom I am proud to call my nieces, and who bring such joy into my life.

Your wife, my sister-in-law, **Maria**, you truly are the gift that made my brother's life complete, and we love you.

Debbie, my cousin, my friend. You were always there for me, even on that first night when I met Michael. If you and I hadn't gone skating, none of this would have been possible, and for that I love you.

DeeDee, through laughter and tears, you were there for me and shared in the joys of me bringing three wonderful daughters into this world. I couldn't have done it without you, and I love you.

Julia, there really are no words to express the friendship and bond the two of us shared. It too, was a gift like no other, and I will always love you for being a very important part of my life.

Jonathan, your memory lives on in your children, and in my heart.

Gail, like an angel whose wings have no limitations or those anonymous footprints in the sand, you were always there for me, and continue to walk by my side. Through it all, you believed in me, and never doubted that the tenacious spirit of me, your stubborn Italian friend, is like that of no other. So, to you my friend, I love you, and I say thank you, for blessing me with your friendship.

Maureen, so dear to my heart. Your unselfish ways, and the many sacrifices you have made for me shine through brilliantly like the North star. Your compassion, ability to bring serenity into any situation, and your ardent sense of humor, continue to astound me. With comfort, I call you Mo, my friend, I love you.

Rhonda, my dear Italian friend, Mama Babushka. Remembering the laughter, tears, the many cups of coffee shared from those cozy little chairs in the local bookstore. Detours in your daily routine, to lend that shoulder to a friend in need. Your friendship, your faith, your benevolent fine qualities, so eternal, from the bottom of my heart, I love you.

Honey, you continue to inspire me with all your astounding qualities. Always believing that every dark cloud does, in fact, have a silver lining. You too have a tenacious spirit. A true friend, wholesome in every way. Thanks for believing in me. Love and hugs to you my friend, forever in my heart.

Jack, I am truly blessed with your friendship and wonderful sense of humor. Through the arduous times in one's life, you have taught me the meaning of God's plan, restored my faith in our Lord, and showed me that miracles really do exist. Thank you for being a special part of our lives and for praying to our almighty Father for healing on my behalf. Love and blessings to you...

And...last but not least, To **Lorraine**, and the rest of my friends that so many times shared another cup of coffee with me from the local café. Your friendships will always be a very special part of my life and I will cherish them forever.

To the many doctors, nurses, and medical professionals that have been by my side, some with compassion, some without. Through all the arduous diagnostics, without you, I wouldn't be here today, to be a part of so many loved ones lives, family and friends alike, who give me unconditional love.

Father, we meet on Sundays, and "Never Give Up" is what you tell us. You are the best there is, a true gift from the heavens. When you speak, we listen. Sometimes it isn't what we want to hear, but we know it's from your heart, and so we believe.

To my editor, **Jessica Keet**, better known to me as Jess. I knew in the very beginning when you came on board as my editor that this collaboration with my story, *That's Another Cup of Coffee* would make me proud. You have taken a heartwarming, yet heart-wrenching story, brought it to life, and turned a dream into a reality. You are truly a professional editor in every sense of the word. Your expertise and quality of work are exceptional. The special attention and precision you pay to detail is just one of the many invaluable qualities you have to offer. Thank you, Jess, and blessings to you, my editor, my friend...

Bob, I never knew that one cup of coffee, such as the one you have designed on the cover of my book, could have such a beautiful representation of all the cups I've had throughout the years. My friend, it is quite evident that you have been blessed with a fine artistic talent; a talent that has captured the essence of my life in the images portrayed. It is a pleasure to have you as a friend, and a privilege to have your handiwork bring my book to life. Thank you for all the countless hours of professional spirit and compassion that went into designing this cover. It's wonderful! Hugs to you, my friend...

Sara Tenaci, yes that would be me. I hope that my courage and tenacious spirit will live on in my children.

1

Roller-skating, to see some guy that was awesome on skates? This was hardly my idea of fun. I could tell this was not going to be your typical Friday night. A friend of mine, Marie, had called and decided that we should go roller-skating that evening, and asked me to meet her at the roller rink. For some unimaginable reason she insisted that I go. I didn't want to go by myself, and in fact, I really didn't want to go at all. After thinking about it for a while, I thought perhaps my cousin, Debbie, would like to join us. The two of us discussed it, and decided that we should go and have some fun.

The parking lot was overloaded with cars. It was literally like "standing room only." Within a few minutes, we found a space, and pulled my little sports car right in. We spotted Marie, who seemed to be bursting at the seams when she saw us. I couldn't quite put my finger on how someone could be so enthusiastic about roller-skating! I introduced Debbie to Marie, and the three of us got into the line to pay, and get our skates. When we got to the front of the line, the attendant was very small in stature, and didn't appear to be too friendly. She was sitting behind what appeared to be a glass wall they called a counter. It had been smudged up, no doubt from all the little fingerprints of their smallest customers.

There was something odd about her, an unearthly look of sorts, and I couldn't figure it out. She had medium-length, light brown, wavy hair, and wore thin wire-rimmed glasses, which magnified the clear, green gaze in her eyes. It was almost as if she could see right through me. Her voice was soft and carried somewhat of an Eastern accent, "Next customer, please..." The atmosphere was definitely colorful, and the theme was Disco. It seemed like there were hundreds of teenyboppers cruising around in roller skates laced halfway up to their knees, driven by four wheels, and the sheer determination to go as fast as possible.

Marie was so excited; she had spotted "Mr.-I-can-do-anything-on-skates." He skated by so fast; it was as if the wind had just picked up, raising the hair on my arms. My goodness, frontward, backward, spinning... Awesome, just like Marie had said. Even though there were literally hundreds of skaters, it did not take me long to set my focus on this one, and he obviously was focused on us, why? I was starting to feel like this was not just some random "Let's go skating this evening," but more of a set up. Did Marie know this guy?

Michael wasn't too tall, less than 6 ft., and what a flirt! He had straight, medium-length, blonde hair, skin as smooth as a baby's bottom, a smile from ear to ear, and piercing green eyes. Kind of cute, and he definitely knew how to skate; this had proved to be a very entertaining evening.

It was fascinating to watch some of the skaters that actually knew what they were doing with those mini-vehicles laced onto their feet we have all come to know as "roller-skates." Around and around they went. Some skaters were going forwards, some backwards, and others were on the floor but not moving at all. Soon I would not be moving either.

It was all together captivating to watch Michael skate, although I was not sure how he managed to skate sporting those tight, black gabardine slacks, which looked more like they had been painted onto his buns of steel. By now, his silk shirt was not so neatly tucked inside his pants and behind his sequined, black leather belt. I felt sure that at any moment he would literally burst at the seams.

Now it was our turn to skate. So, out into the crazy commute of skaters zooming by we went. Between my heart pounding from the nerves, and my legs wobbling, I was a wreck. It took me a while to get into the swing of things. As I came around the turn by the DJ booth, the strobe lights were flashing with a blaze of colors like a thunderstorm lighting up the sky.

Since I was not paying that much attention to what I was doing, I didn't realize that someone had stopped right in my path. Ah! Of course, I didn't think to stop like a normal person. What was normal? These skaters were moonstruck. I lost my balance, and felt my body reel from side to side, right before it settled onto the unforgiving, hardwood floor.

At that moment, I thought my legs were broken. I could no longer see those gleaming green eyes, or those buns of steel. All I could focus on was the dreadful pain I was now feeling, and the embarrassment of being such a klutz.

Everyone continued to skate past me except for "Mr. Fancy Footwork" himself. He probably planted the other skater there, so that I could fall. If you ask me, this entire evening was much too coincidental; just like in a fairytale. Yeah, right, I was swept off my feet. Michael rushed over, picked me up off the floor, and carried me out into the lounge area. I couldn't believe this had just happened! I was very humiliated, to say the least. What next, a pumpkin carriage pulled by horses?

Once all had settled down, we introduced ourselves. He told me his name was Michael Tenaci. Now, with a much closer look, his eyes were a bright, emerald green, and he did have smooth, rosy cheeks like a baby's butt, just as Marie had said. But how old was this guy? Either he did a good job of shaving, or he didn't even have peach fuzz on his face.

I thought that Marie must be out of her mind to want me to meet some guy that was obviously no more than eighteen years old! Michael and I continued to talk; you know the small talk "third degree stuff" that goes on when you meet someone for the first time. He told me that he was twenty-three. Okay, I thought to myself. What is this guy smoking? There was no way that he was twenty-three, and I was not going to be skating around with some flirt that looked young enough to still be in High School. It just wasn't right. After all, I had just turned twenty-six, an old woman!

Michael could tell that I was not convinced, and had to see for myself. So, he took out his wallet, and showed me his ID. Well, he really was twenty-three. I was amazed. *"All right, you win, I will skate with you,"* I said. Still a bit of an age difference but not too bad, at least I wouldn't be robbing the cradle.

Michael was all smiles, and Marie's little plan seemed to have worked out for them. She and Debbie went about their business, skating with everyone else, and left Michael and I to get to know each other. Once my legs felt as if they were still connected, we decided to go out and start skating once again. We were all having so much fun. Michael showed me how to skate as a pair, with him skating backwards.

Wouldn't you know it, the DJ had to play a mushy song. Was this a setup too? We skated to a song by Peaches and Herb called *I Dedicate My Love to you*. Everyone else in the arena continued to skate, but while the two of us skated as a couple, time stood still. We held each other close as if we had known each other for years. It was all too comfortable... there seemed to be a body chemistry building in unison. My heart was pounding as the two of us skated, holding our bodies close together. It seemed like a dream. I couldn't explain this sensation. This didn't happen in real life, did it?

There we were, face to face, as if in rapture, holding each other with our hot, sweaty hands, and an intense feeling of warmth and security surrounding our two bodies as we continued to skate as one. It seemed as if we were the only ones on the floor. I wasn't even sure how I kept skating. I don't remember my body moving, let alone my feet skating. All I can remember is the piercing look from his bright, emerald green eyes gazing deeply into mine. What was this? How did this happen? Had fate brought us here, or was it Marie?

Apparently the song had ended long before Michael & I realized it had. In some unimaginable way, we had managed to get lost in each other's eyes. I had been looking straight into those emerald greens; it was like lying down in a field of mile-high green grass, on a warm spring day, with a feeling of pure serenity.

The evening ended better than what any of us had expected. Marie went on home, and Michael made arrangements to meet me back at Debbie's house, where we would drop her off, and then meet somewhere for drinks. We had invited

Debbie, but she thought it would be in our best interests if it were just the two of us.

We met at the Towers, which was a bar and grill of sorts, with dancing. When I arrived, Michael was being a Good Samaritan, and helping someone get into their car after they had locked themselves out. Once inside, we found ourselves a cozy, little table for two in a dimly lit area, and ordered a soda. The music wasn't soothing but more of something that made the adrenaline really pump. That was all right because we didn't want to dance, we just wanted to talk, and enjoy each other's company.

In the midst of our conversation, Michael asked for my phone number. I gave it to him with the hopes that he would, in fact, call me. However I assumed he wouldn't, and that he'd probably lose my number. This was too good to be true. If all first impressions were right, he certainly was a gentleman, and different from most guys I had dated. I had never met anyone with such diverse qualities.

We both felt it was time to leave. He walked me to my car and opening my door, told me that he would give me a call. No, we did not make mad, passionate love in the parking lot; not even a kiss. After all, this was not even a regular date. We both went our separate ways. As I drove home with my mind still in somewhat of a fog as to what had transpired that night, I thought to myself, *"I might never see him again... What if he doesn't call me?"* I could only hope that he was not like all the rest.

2

When I got home, I started to think about my last date prior to meeting Michael. It was a blind date, and he picked me up outfitted in something very similar to what a clown would wear. Nothing matched. He was about 5' 5", and somewhat dumpy with black, unruly hair. His glasses were thick with broad, black frames to cover his big, brown eyes. The outfit had to be a joke; no one could put an outfit together as he did. He wore a light blue plaid shirt, with some sort of multicolor, abstract, misfit bowtie. Pinstriped floods with cuffs that I guess he thought were pants. The socks were definitely argyle.

Well, I couldn't tell him to leave based on his apparel, so I was stuck with him for at least one date. I knew from the beginning that this was going to be a very lengthy evening. This guy was definitely anomalous in every sense of the word. We went to dinner at a restaurant that had peanut shells scattered over the entire floor. We had absolutely nothing in common. George insisted on sharing with me the fact that he thought black roses were very romantic.

My watch became very important to me, and I could not wait for him to take me home. It had been the most appalling date. The comparison between that guy and Michael was... well, there was no comparison. I had only hoped that Michael would call... day and night, all I could think about was that evening I had met Michael and the wonderful sensation I felt while with him. I wanted to get lost in his eyes, his arms, again. I wondered if he had felt the same way I did. Several days had passed, and it seemed hopeless that Michael would call me. I was beginning to think I was destined to date circus acts. Suddenly the phone rang, and it was Michael. I was elated.

We talked on the phone for hours, and made plans to date. Michael came over every evening after work, and on weekends. When he wasn't with me, or at work, he would be talking to me on the phone into the wee hours of the morning.

Neither of us had an extravagant or materialistic lifestyle. Going out to see a movie, or getting something light to eat was acceptable for both of us. At times, just cuddling next to each other on the sofa, or going out for a nice drive was what we enjoyed most together.

After dating for almost a month, Michael and I went to a restaurant called Peppermill. He was different that night, and I couldn't quite put a finger on why. His hands were sweating again, like that first night we had skated together. It was as if someone had plugged him in.

That night he was dressed exceptionally well with another pair of his form-fitting steel blue, gabardine slacks, and a matching blue pinstriped silk shirt. Every hair on his head seemed to be in place.

He was now sporting something under his nose that initially resembled peach fuzz, but was now really starting to look like a mustache. His aftershave gave off a clean, fresh, most inviting, scent.

The restaurant was full, however Michael didn't mind because this was all part of his plan. While awaiting your table, you sit in the candlelit lounge on cozy, little sofas by the crackling fire, with the faint sound of piano music playing in the background.

The atmosphere is everything, especially when you are with someone you feel like you are falling in love with. Michael, a hopeless romantic, just seemed too good to be true.

As we sat on the sofa, snuggled up close in front of the hot, blazing fire, it felt as if we too were burning together. Once again I was lost in his green eyes, which sparkled with the glow of the fire. His soft, smooth cheeks had already pinked up. While sipping from a glass of wine, and enjoying being in each other's arms, Michael decided he had something to ask me. Once again, I thought, *"Oh no, he is like the rest of the jerks, and is going to ask me to go back to his place for a roll in the hay. Has he been playing me for a fool?"*

Much to my surprise, he started to talk about plans, plans which would include me. Once again, Michael had managed to surprise me, unlike anyone I had ever been with before. By now, I felt like I was burning up. I was not sure if it was the wine, the heat from the fire, or the heat in my heart. With his next question, I had a good idea of where Michael wanted our relationship to go.

I took a big gulp, instead of a small sip of wine, and listened intently to what he had to say next. With his eyes sparkling like fire, he looked into mine, and asked me how many children I wanted. Had he just asked me what I thought he had? He waited patiently for my reply. *"I would like three, how about you?"* I said.

His response was the same. Just as we were about to get further into this conversation, the hostess came to let us know our table was ready. I could have cuddled with him on that sofa, next to the crackling of the luminous fire, all evening, without even going into the dining area at all.

The dining area was nice, but the atmosphere was different now; not as cozy and intimate. Michael and I both enjoyed indulging in the simple pleasures of a mouth-watering prime rib dinner, which included an oversize baked potato overflowing with butter, sour cream and chives, asparagus and a delicious deep green, spinach salad. Dinner was delicious, and I knew that I didn't have too much room left in my tummy for dessert. However, who in their right mind could pass up dessert? We both ordered the chocolate mousse, with a generous portion of whipped cream on top. It was delectable, just as the entire evening had been. Neither of us had wanted the evening to end, but all good things must come to an end, temporarily at least, but not before being sealed with a succulent goodnight kiss, and an abundance of passion. The kind of passion you would want to last a lifetime.

3

It was a beautiful sunny afternoon, and there was an irresistible aroma of fresh garlic, basil, and homegrown tomatoes simmering in the kitchen. It must be Mom's Italian pasta and meatballs. Over on the butcher block I could see three loaves of fresh, homemade bread with steam still rising from their delectable, golden brown crusts- just asking for someone to cut a slice, and spread a generous dollop of butter on top. On the other hand, maybe some pecorino grating cheese, extra virgin olive oil, and a dash of salt and pepper. It looked like our dinner was going to be scrumptious. My mouth was already starting to water.

I had just finished showering and drying my hair, and decided to sit at the kitchen table to paint my nails. I also had this weird hair stocking on my head. With naturally curly hair such as mine, after you blow it dry and look like you have been caught in a tornado, then top that off by burning it a bit with the curling iron, you have to put some type of cap on to calm it down, with hopes you won't frighten anyone. We call my cap "horns" because it does, in fact, stick up like horns.

Well, wouldn't you know it? My timing was always flawless... but not this time. My night in shining armor just decided to make an unexpected early evening visit. *"Oh, my goodness!*

"What is he going to think when he sees me looking like this?" Michael couldn't have cared less what I had on my head. He seemed to be in a euphoric state of mind, and I don't think he even noticed. *"Hi, Michael, it's nice to see you. My, you look like you are in a very good mood!"* He said, "This is for you," and handed me an adorable little box, wrapped in glossy white paper, with a delicate silver bow on top. No, I thought to myself. He couldn't have, there was no way... *"Michael?"* He just looked at me with this unbelievable smile, and said, "Well, aren't you going to open it?" I had to admit, it did look the slightest bit suspicious! I looked at my parents, and I don't think they knew what to do or say except... "Open it!"

So, without further ado, I proceeded to open my adorable little box. *"Oh, my God, Michael!"* Yes, it was an engagement ring. I couldn't believe it. I got up, wet polish on my nails, and horns intact, to indulge myself in a big hug, and luscious kiss. I guess Michael realized after the hug and kiss that I was elated, and with that I said, *"Yes, I will marry you!"*

Obviously, Michael had not used the traditional method of proposing. He hadn't even asked, or discussed it with my parents, but after all, I was already twenty-six. Once I had unglued myself from him, I took a glance over at my parents. By all appearances, they had slipped into shock. I think all the blood had run out of their veins, and they looked like they had just seen a ghost. It is hard to describe... They suddenly looked like the plague had just dropped in. It took a while, but then they actually started to move about the kitchen with a bit of excitement, and finally congratulated the two of us.

My brother, Tony, was in Clear Lake building a house so we thought it might be a good idea to call, and give him the good news. I must admit, he was not all too thrilled. After all, when he had left in the early summer, I had not even met Michael yet. In addition, being the Mafia type that he is, he would have wanted to give him the third degree before allowing me to accept a marriage proposal. Therefore, against his unknown judgment and with much apprehension, he congratulated us.

While Dad ran to the store to purchase champagne and beer, I got on the phone and started to call my close family and friends. There were mixed feelings amongst all of them. I sensed a combination from them of shock, "Let's have her committed," "She's finally in love," and then finally "Congratulations!" I have no doubt that no one expected an engagement announcement that soon. We invited them all over to join us for a glass of champagne to celebrate our wonderful news, where we not only announced our engagement, but set our wedding date as well. June 6, 1981 was the day we chose to become husband and wife.

The hours had passed and I was still in shock, to say the least. I was thinking, *"Pinch me quick, I must be dreaming...*" But, we were really all there, and it was a dream, a dream come true. We played some music to add to the celebration. Yes, we had all of the women in tears when Michael wanted to play the song we first skated to together; *I Dedicate My Love to You.*

Realizing now that we had a future together brought us both a feeling of bliss. We had so many things to take care of in preparation for our marriage, as well as for our wedding day; of course, the majority of the preparation for the wedding day is done by the bride-to-be herself.

Both of us continued to work at our current jobs. I was working at a check printing company doing data entry for all the banks, and Michael was actually working for a bank. My co-workers were so astonished as to how two people had fallen in love so quickly. However, they told me they had known I was falling in love when they saw the glow on my face, and the sparkle in my eyes. This was one of the first signs. They were all very happy for us. They would always get a kick out of all the flowers and gifts that Michael would have sent to me at work.

It was a beautiful Sunday afternoon, and Michael had decided that it was time to take me to meet his family, although I couldn't understand why he seemed so apprehensive about it. However, that did become obvious when we arrived at the house.

Remember the unearthly lady behind the counter at the roller rink? The one with the clear, green gaze in her eyes? Well, ironically, that was Michael's mother. And Michael had told me earlier in the week that his Mom was clairvoyant, which would explain the eerie look on her face when I paid my admission to skate; she knew before I did that her son and I would meet, and that he would propose.

It is somewhat distressing to be in the presence of someone that can read your mind and/or see things happening. Nevertheless, for now, we won't go there.

Michael's mom welcomed us into her home where all his siblings seemed to be eagerly awaiting our arrival. I was introduced to all of them by Michael. Well, actually only four of them because one wasn't there. They seemed receptive to my being there, but acted strangely with Michael; almost as if they were making fun of him, and I could see that it was making him extremely uncomfortable.

Michael had told me on the way to the house that his family didn't care for him all that much. I found it hard to believe and wondered why no one could love this wonderful man, this gentle man with a heart of gold. The man I fell in love with. Now, I could see what he had been telling me about them. They were crude with him. I personally didn't like the way they seemed to be poking fun at him. I just couldn't understand it.

One of his sisters made a wisecrack remark that Michael should be walking the strip downtown. What was she implying? So, I asked her, and it was quite simple; at least they thought it was. Michael's maternal uncle was gay, and coincidentally, Michael looked exactly like him, therefore, in the kids' eyes, that made him gay as well. Was this guilt by association? I thought it was ludicrous, and very disrespectful.

In the short amount of time we visited, his family painted a very abstract picture of what Michael's family life was like. We didn't meet Michael's father because no one actually knew where he was. Apparently, he had left Michael's mother with the first three of the six kids when Michael was a toddler. Michael was told that his father was in the Marines, and had gone AWOL. She also told her son, Michael, that if he ever tried to find his father she would disown him. If you ask me, it was very mysterious.

Nevertheless, I didn't know the family well enough to make a judgment, and it really wasn't any of my business to pursue the issue. I just couldn't imagine that though, a mother telling her son that wanted to know his father's whereabouts that she would disown him. What had happened? Was he a murderer, rapist, what? Was she covering up for herself? Had she done something she didn't want the kids to know about?

SARA TENACI
THAT'S ANOTHER CUP OF COFFEE

4

Even though I was not literally marrying Michael's family, it bothered me to see how they treated him. I was starting to see, as with all relationships, what impact his family had on him, most of which was not so good. They had destroyed his self-esteem. I could not fathom what their problem was. He was such a gentlemen, and always respectful with everyone, and just brimming with astounding qualities, which I greatly admired.

The wedding plans were coming along and keeping us all busy. Michael was involved with the planning, however was at work most of the day while we were getting things organized. I was also still working but had a little more free time then he did. We had already chosen the bridal party, which was going to be just under two dozen including bridesmaids, ushers, ring boys, flower girls etc.

Winter was near, and the weather was changing. The air was now quite chilly and time to bundle up. Michael and I would often spend evenings sitting in the living room snuggled up on the sofa, close to the luminous fire ablaze in the fireplace. He was having some problems with an agonizing back pain, and he would always enjoy me giving him back rubs. Now who wouldn't? A couple in love, sitting by a cozy fire, with a robust desire for the two to become one.

The backaches continued, and I really became quite concerned. I wondered why his back was always hurting so much. Since I was going to be his wife and he was going to be a big part of my life, I thought I should ask.

So I did ask, and there was something he had been keeping from me. Evidently, several months prior to us meeting, he was driving into the city one evening for the bank, and was involved in a horrific automobile accident. *"Oh, my God, Michael! Why didn't you tell me?"*

It was no wonder his back was always giving him trouble. Michael said, "I didn't want you to worry."

As I sat close, giving him yet another back rub, he started to tell me about the accident. I was horrified about what had happened and what he had to endure. He explained that the other car had run into him with such an enormous impact that it had crushed the front of his car, leaving him trapped in between the front seat and the dash. Now, I could understand why his back was hurting so much; he was lucky to be alive.

I asked him who was responsible for his care, and medical expenses and he told me that the bank, his employer, was taking full responsibility for all the medical bills and damages. He also told me that they were working on a settlement with him. *"Well,"* I said. *"At least you can get some physical therapy, and rehabilitate your back."*

Our relationship seemed to be flourishing every day, and our wedding day was drawing nearer. Three months had passed, and Michael was still having lots of trouble with his back. I was giving him countless back rubs, which didn't seem to be doing any good, with the exception of us just enjoying being close to one another. I was becoming increasingly alarmed by this situation, and couldn't figure out why the bank hadn't sent him for physical therapy yet.

Michael had been coming to my house every evening after work. He would have his clean clothes with him, take showers there, and join us for dinner. My parents were okay with this; it wasn't as if we were taking showers together. Heaven forbid...

One evening, Michael came over and said that he had spoken with his supervisors at work regarding the accident. They had told him that they were working out the details of a settlement, and that he would be getting it soon. I was pleased to hear this because he would finally be able to get some therapy, and pay the medical bills. I said, *"Michael, you could have been killed in that accident, and we would have never met. It's time they took care of you and your back."*

Michael had never really had much in his life, and I certainly hadn't fallen in love with him for his money, because he didn't have any. I fell in love with the man. My family had really taken him under their wing, and did everything for him. We certainly were not a wealthy family from a monetary standpoint, but we were a lot better off than his family.

My dad was a contractor, and his Mom was working her buns off trying to support the other five siblings, as well as being on welfare.

The back problem started to become a major issue, which was getting way out of control. Michael was not going for any physical therapy, and I was really starting to worry. How much pain did the guy have to experience before they decided to send him for therapy?

He would continuously come home, and tell me that the bank was getting closer to settling with him.

That was it! I had had enough of these back massages! I said, *"You need a therapist for this back. My back rubs don't seem to be helping you at all!"* They were obviously just jerking him around, and had been for much too long. What was the matter with these people? Considering I was about to become his wife, I had decided to call the bank and see just who was in charge of this ridiculous situation. I would talk to Michael and tell him that I planned to call to get this situation straightened up for him so that he could get some therapy.

Michael had finally had enough of the bank, and was offered a job in construction with my family. I thought to myself, *"How is he going to work in construction with his back always giving him such excruciating pain?"*

He didn't want me to worry too much, and didn't think it would be a good idea for me to get involved with calling the bank on his behalf. For reasons I wasn't clear on, he got extremely upset with me when I told him that I was going to call the bank. It seemed like now that he wasn't working for the bank any longer, they were just going to let this settlement, and his therapy, fizzle out.

I didn't want to be responsible for medical expenses that they should be paying, and I certainly didn't want Michael to have to deal with major back pain all his life. The days and weeks seemed to be flying by, and Michael's back condition seemed to be deteriorating... That was it! I was calling the bank! I was not about to see him in constant back pain, and I certainly didn't want to be his "Massage Queen!"

I got on the phone, and called the bank. I introduced myself and told them why I was calling. The first customer service girl didn't really know what I was talking about, and transferred me to the branch manager. I don't recall her name, but it became one of the most disturbing conversations I have ever had in my entire life! *"What the hell? You're kidding me? He did what?"* I just couldn't believe my ears; I was totally outraged

My heart suddenly felt as if it had been ripped out of my chest, and my emotions and feelings were running rampant. Anger started to build, and the shock settled in. The tears began to flow, and envelop my face. I felt as if someone had just pulled the plug on my blood supply, and drained every drop I had left in my body.

With whom had I fallen in love? This had to be a nightmare. This couldn't be happening! I fell in love with this man, and I was marrying him? How could anyone stoop this low?

By now the branch manager was very apologetic, and really didn't know what to do or say, considering Michael and I were engaged to be married soon. I thanked her for her time, and apologized for having bothered her. What was I going to do? This couldn't be Michael; there must be some mistake! My Michael would not do this.

To sum it up concisely, it went something like this. I had found out that my future husband, the man I was so deeply in love with, was a low life bastard! He had been playing a game, which might cost him our marriage, and any future with me. He had been lying to me for several months with regard to his accident!

You know, the one in which he was so severely injured? The one that the bank was, beyond any doubt, going to be responsible for all the medical expenses and therapy? Well, guess what? The bank wasn't responsible for any of his therapy or medical expenses; they had no intention of settling with him then, or ever.

5

And why not? Because there was NO accident! My night in shining armor and dream come true, had fabricated the entire story! The branch manager had conveyed to me that Michael had never been injured on the job, nor had there ever been an automobile accident involving him and the bank. My head now felt like a volcano with the steam bellowing out, ready to erupt.

There had to be something wrong with him. What kind of person did something so preposterous? He made me, his fiancée, think that he was in such excruciating pain, just so that he could have his back massaged.... Was that how he wanted to get attention? Was that how he showed me that he loved me, by lying to me? What kind of asshole was I marrying?

It was a really bright and beautiful day out, but not for me. It suddenly became very gloomy. I felt like there had been a death. Actually, there had been a death; the death of what I believed to be so pure and true, a love that couldn't be eradicated. I had to get out of the house. I ran out of the house and into the backyard, pacing back and forth, not knowing what to do next.

How was I going to confront him when he came home from work that evening? By then, I was beyond upset, and my emotions were out of control. I felt so betrayed that without even giving him the benefit of the doubt, I wanted to just call the whole engagement and wedding off. How could I marry someone who had totally fabricated such an appalling story? Had he no shame? Why had he done this to me? Was I that much of a pushover? I guess he figured I loved him enough that this wouldn't matter?

I had decided that when he got home and we were by ourselves, I was going to mention the accident, and see where he went with it. A couple hours later, Michael came in from a hard day's work in construction. I tried desperately not to explode, and waited patiently for everyone to go about their business, so that Michael and I could be alone. This time being alone didn't mean passionate hugs and kisses, or those not-so-needed back massages.

Michael was acting his usual happy-as-a-lark self. My family had gone out, and Michael thought that we were going to sit down and cozy up. I thought, *"Yeah, right, you low life piece of shit!"* Funny how you can be so in love with someone, and yet be so overwhelmed with anger that you suddenly loathe the sight of them.

He started to tell me about his day, and I tried to be receptive. I started my conversation with regard to the bank, and how I thought it was time he cleared this matter up. The time wasn't right for him, and he started to tell me a little bit more bullshit about how he had, once again, spoken to the bank.

Yes, this was my cue. I said, *"Michael, you are the most full of shit person I have ever met in my entire life!"* He played dumb and responded with, "What do you mean?" I said, *"You know exactly what I mean, you asshole!"* I don't even swear, but this changed everything!

How can you yell at someone when you are almost frothing at the mouth, without swearing? Are you supposed to say, *"Michael, darling, you made a little booboo and we need to fix it? You have been naughty, now go to your room"*? This was an adult about to get married! Right now, there were so many things running circles inside my head that I couldn't keep up. There were many, many things that I would have liked to call him and trust me, none of which were precious and none of which included, *"I love you, Michael, I can't wait to become husband and wife, so that we can make mad, passionate love together!"*

As I tried to make eye contact with him, I began to impersonate how he was always moaning about his back injury; you could see the color changes in his face, which were similar to that of a spinning color wheel. The mood was suddenly somber. You could tell he didn't know what to expect. I said, *"Michael, I called your bank today and found out that there never was any accident! You fabricated the entire story!"* He was speechless. All those different colors his face had just turned were gone; he was stone cold white. There wasn't anything in the world that he could say that was going to change the way I was feeling at that moment. He started to whine, and tell me how sorry he was and I said, *"Save it for your next Bimbo! Our wedding is off!"*

This would be our first, and probably our last, argument. He pleaded with me not to call our wedding off and said, "Please let me explain!" I said, *"How do you explain something so stupid and insensitive?"* He said, "I didn't have anything to offer you, and I wanted you to think that I had something to bring into our future. I figured if I told you I had money, that you would love me more."

"What? You have got to be kidding; you really are an ass with a capital 'A', aren't you? Where did you get such an idiotic idea? Do you just make things up as you go? When I met you, I didn't ask if you had money, nor did I care! I didn't care what kind of car you drove; I didn't care about any of those material things. I fell in love with you! Can't you see that? I wasn't a gold digger. I knew you didn't have anything, and that didn't matter. All that mattered was that I thought you were this wonderful man that I had fallen in love with, and the rest we would work for together. Michael, the sad thing here is, you wanted me to feel sorry for you. What is that? And I actually did, Michael, but I will never feel sorry for you another day in your entire life!"

I look back now on all the times I had felt so sorry for him, and massaged his back. Was I crazy? Why didn't I see this coming? As far as I was concerned, he was as phony as a three-dollar bill. As the days seemed to slowly creep along, the two of us were miserable. I really missed being in his arms, and sharing my life with him, and I knew, or at least I thought I knew, that he felt the same way, but he had planted that little seed of doubt in the back of my mind. Everything thus far had been really wonderful, until then.

This situation was either going to make our relationship stronger, or it was going to be the end of it. We discussed this for days, and he continued to plead with me not to call off our engagement, or wedding. He said, "I know now this was a stupid thing to do, and I promise you here and now, I will never lie to you again! Just please let me prove it to you."

I said, *"All right, Michael, I will give you another chance, maybe you can turn this into a positive experience. I hope that you have learned a valuable lesson from this, but maybe not, we shall see. However, let me tell you something, buster! Don't you ever expect to get any kind of pity from me, EVER! You blew it! You pretended to be in excruciating pain, and now I will never be able to tell when you are hurting or not. Do you know what this does to me for trusting you?"* All he said was, "Let me make it up to you, I love you, and I want to be your husband." We managed to move forward, and I tried to put this incident behind me as just one of those insane things that happen in relationships.

6

It was a New Year, 1981, the one in which Michael and I were to be married. In less than six months, I would become Mrs. Sara Tenaci. Our relationship seemed to be blooming once again. So far, Michael had kept his promise. I thought that perhaps he really had learnt his lesson. This would be an extremely busy year for all of us, and we were all hoping for a healthy, happy, and prosperous one. Family and friends were all enjoying helping us with our wedding preparations.

Being engaged to be married was probably one of the most exciting things that had ever happened in my life. I was in love, real love that would last forever. I had a man that was truly devoted to me, and I knew that he loved me with all of his heart.

It was anything but a typical weekday; my family and I were extremely nervous while waiting for the doctor to call with my brother's blood test results. The air in our house was as thick as a gloomy winter's fog, and filled with worry. In the past few weeks, he had been feeling lethargic, and was overcome with frequent night sweats.

Also, there appeared to be something seriously wrong with his neck, as it was becoming quite large. They had run numerous tests on him, but nothing conclusive had shown up until that day.

You know when you just get that gut feeling that the phone is going to ring with bad news? Well, by mid afternoon the phone did, in fact, ring. Although eager to answer it with hopes we would hear good news, every one of us was too overwhelmed with fear to pick it up.

With much apprehension, my dad finally decided that he should pick up the phone. It was the doctor's office calling. As my dad stood there listening to the doctor on the other end, we watched his usual bright smile fade, his olive, Italian skin turn very pale, and his radiant, hazel eyes start to tear up.

He was completely speechless, and listening very intently to what the doctor was telling him. We were all trying to read his expressions, and they made it obvious that it was not good news. He thanked the doctor for calling, and hung up the phone.

Just as we figured, the news was not good. As my brother stood there waiting to hear the news, he too knew that it wasn't good. "Cancer," my dad said. "You've got Hodgkin's Disease."

As you can imagine, my brother didn't know what to say or do. He was in total shock, and my mom went completely hysterical. Although we were all upset, my dad tried to comfort my brother, while my aunts and I took care of my mom, who was screaming, throwing up, and passing out all at the same time. It was like a nightmare. Something you never want to live through; more like something you see on a soap opera, and cry your eyes out watching.

I guess God just gives you the strength to do what you have to, in order to get through a crisis such as this. It was so difficult for me to learn that my baby brother had been diagnosed with cancer at the age of only twenty-three. All I kept thinking was, *"Oh, my God, is he going to die?"* It was devastating, and I think my body and mind just became numb. I had to kick it into gear, and pull myself together to be there for my whole family. Michael hadn't come home from work yet, so he didn't know.

As the day drew to a close, and the house had become a little quieter, we had to call the doctor's office to find out about treatments. He was going to have to undergo several more tests, and surgery for staging of the cancer. The next few weeks were horrific. This was probably one of the most difficult things any of us would ever have to endure, especially my brother. Although we always prayed, we did even more praying during this heavyhearted time in our lives. The tests and surgeries were physically and mentally exhausting for him, as well as mentally draining on the rest of us. After having had his surgery for staging, the results showed a stage two. Not good by any means, but at least there was hope.

He was going to have to undergo radiation therapy for a few months. We all pulled together with all our love, and supported each other. The love and the bond that we all shared helped us to keep ourselves together, and helped support him during this most difficult period in his, and our, lives. It took some time for all of us to come to terms with the cancer issue, but we had to try our best not to be consumed by it.

What had happened to our wedding plans? Oh, yeah, we were getting married. Well, that obviously had to be put aside for the time being. Hearing the sad news put a damper on our wedding plans, and it had to be shoved under the rug for a while.

Eventually, we got back into the swing of things again. My mom, dad, and brother, did not want this to get in the way of our wedding plans. Timing was never right with cancer. This was a very traumatic time in all of our lives, but we had to pull together, and be strong.

Of course Michael was also upset to hear my brother had cancer. However, the two of them had never bonded. Michael was never good enough for my brother, and given the fact he had never met him when we became engaged, he hadn't liked him from the first day he did meet him.

As the months passed by, we did the best we could at having a normal life. The radiation seemed to be working, and it looked like my brother was going to beat the cancer. This was the best news we had heard all year. Michael and I could finally try to get back into enjoying our engagement. For a long time we actually felt guilty feeling happy about our relationship; it was as if it were forbidden.

Our relationship was as strong as ever, and had already weathered a couple of storms. Wedding plans were once again underway, and we finally were back to enjoying all the showers, parties, and preparations that come with an engagement. We certainly had our work cut out for us now with playing catch up.

It was a beautiful sunny day, and the air was fresh and full of love. Michael and I had the most invigorating feeling, as our wedding plans were making favorable progress. We had been invited over to my cousins that afternoon. They were expecting us at their house around noon, to participate in more pre-wedding activities. When we arrived, there didn't seem to be anything unusual, with the exception of many cars being parked in their neighborhood.

Indeed, pre-wedding activities. We went to the front door, and Michael had me knock to go in first. This should have tipped me off. My cousin came to the door, let me in, and there was a sudden burst of voices, yelling, "Surprise!" It was, in fact, my bridal shower, and what a surprise it was. I never realized just how many friends and relatives we had.

They were lined up by the dozen, it seemed. I was delighted to see everyone, and so overwhelmed that this was a shower for me, the bride-to-be. No men allowed, so Michael went on his way to join the rest of the men in our family at my parents' house.

I stumbled, or should I say floated, through the day; it was like being on a cloud, to greet my guests, and share congratulatory hugs and kisses with everyone. I had to stop for a moment and try to absorb all the warmth and beauty that filled the house. Everyone was dressed up in their semi-formal attire, and looked lovely; you could just sense the excitement in the air.

I could hear voices and laughter everywhere. Discussions about the wedding; outfits, hairdos, and food! And there was so much food at the party.

Everything looked scrumptious; the aroma of fresh homemade lasagna in the oven made my mouth water, big juicy meatballs bathing inside a deep red sauce with that sensational smell of garlic and basil, in a colossal saucepan simmering on the stove. A variety of homemade pizzas, with generous portions of sausage, cheese, mushrooms, anchovies, and olives, cut and piled high on serving trays lined up on the dining table. Mouth watering potato, macaroni, and green salads. Oh, and the Jell-O salads! Who would have thought that Jell-O could look so tempting? Grandma's famous multicolor, and flavored Jell-

O cut into perfect little squares, and mixed with cool whip, juicy wedges of pineapple, and other family secrets, beautifully displayed in a sunburst bowl surrounded with ladyfingers.

Lots of mouthwatering roast beef, ham, turkey, salami, provolone, Swiss, American, and cheddar cheeses. Rolls, hundreds of them, stacked high. There were nuts, chips, mints, and countless other delectable goodies just waiting for us to try. Plenty to quench your thirst including a bowl of sparkling, ruby red punch, with a delicate fog rising out of the center- dry ice, sherbet, and champagne, which resembled an erupting volcano. And let's not forget the cake; it was enormous and stunning, with 'Congratulations' decorations. A white, luscious cake filled with rum custard, and enveloped with a blanket of thick, delicious, pearl white whipped cream, as flavorsome as that of pure heaven.

Gifts, mountains of elegantly wrapped gifts, with glossy white, silver, and assorted pastel papers, draped with wedding bell decor, and beautiful satin ribbons and bows. Everything was beautiful, and all that a newlywed couple could ever want or need. We played many games under the influence of just a slight amount of the bubbling champagne. It was a most memorable day for all of us, especially me, and it will last a lifetime in my heart.

7

Spring was in the air, and you could see beautiful, green trees with colorful blossoms opening up, in all shapes and sizes. Little squirrels were running up the branches, and the flowers were consuming the brilliant sunshine in all their glory, with a rainbow of colors everywhere. With spring came many beautiful things, one of which included a lingerie shower given by my bridesmaids.

We had a wonderful time. I must have received more than a dozen suggestive gowns, and they were all gorgeous. There were long, flowing silky gowns, short baby dolls, and some without bottoms! Michael was going to really enjoy intimate moments with these... Especially one in particular that was a big hit with all the ladies. My best friend, Julia, gave me a "Black Teddy." You know the ones that snap and unsnap under your bottom? As I held it up, my face felt like it was on fire; there was some serious blushing happening there. After all, I was used to good, old, oversized flannels, bottoms and tops, with socks - all of which came from one of our favorite family department stores - and none of this fancy, sensuous type of lingerie.

Everyone found it very amusing and thought it would be a great idea to wear the "Black Teddy" for the Honeymoon. I had a feeling this was going to become Michael's favorite as well... My sleep attire had just taken a step forward from "the girl next door in flannels" to "Victoria's Secret crotchless designs..."

As the wedding drew nearer, it seemed that every day there was more to take care of. My mom and I were doing almost everything now, since Michael had done pretty much all he could for a while, with the exception of spending quality time with me, his future bride. Extravagance was not essential for Michael and I. We were completely content with just going out to a movie, or for an ice cream. As it was getting warmer, we were not lighting fires anymore, but most often we could be found snuggled up like two teddy bears on the sofa, creating our own lusty fire.

Michael and I were not only going to be married, but we had also become best friends. We always found great pleasure in spending lots of quality time together. It was almost like we were one, and no one else existed. The two of us had such a strong desire to be more intimate with each other, but we knew that we had promised to wait until we were husband and wife.

Julia and I had been best friends for most of our lives; actually we were more like sisters. She thought it might be a good idea for the two of us to go on an overnight bus trip to Reno, which we did. Michael was going to have to work anyway, and he thought it would be a great idea for Julia and I to have a little fun together. You know, some girl talk...

After spending the day in Reno, and having more fun than you could imagine, we went back to our motel. Oddly enough for this time of year, it was raining, and I don't mean a couple of sprinkles; it was pouring, and very cold.

Considering our accommodations were not like staying at the Ritz, we did not have a phone in our room, and I had promised Michael that I would call him. Consequently, Julia and I had to run down the street around midnight, in the pouring rain, and chilled to the bone. I must have been crazy to be running around in downtown Reno, at midnight, to look for a phone booth? Was that what love did to you?

Michael had told me that he would be home after work, and had no plans to do anything else except wait for my call, and then await my return with open arms. Finally, Julia and I found a phone booth sitting in about a foot of water. Our clothes were drenched and our hair, well with us both having naturally curly hair, you can imagine what it looked like. We didn't care, we just wanted to call Michael, and get back to the motel before we got mugged. I called Michael and much to my surprise, he was not home. I let the phone ring innumerable times with no luck. Therefore, I tried again thinking that I had the wrong number. Still, no one answered... Hmmm.... where was he at midnight? I hoped nothing had happened to him. Maybe he was sound asleep, and didn't hear the phone? This was unusual. Well, there wasn't much I could do about it, so Julia and I ran back to our motel.

We arrived home the next day. Michael and I were so happy to see each other; you would have thought we had been apart for months, instead of a little over one day. I said, *"By the way, Michael, I called you a couple of times last night around midnight. Why didn't you answer the phone?"* His reply was that he did not hear the phone ring at all, and that I had probably dialed the wrong number. He said that he hadn't left his house all evening. That was interesting, I knew I had dialed the right number. Oh, well, at least nothing had happened to him.

Our family and friends had been amazing with all that they were doing to help us get ready for our wedding day; I don't think we could have done it without everyone's love and support. Most of my family were really delighted that Michael and I were about to be married, and everyone had waited a long time for this day to come. Our wedding had become the main event in all our lives, and we couldn't have been happier. I think the entire family went out and bought dazzling new outfits for our special day. There was no doubt in my mind that this would be a very special and most memorable day for all of us.

Just when I thought I had had all my showers and parties, I got a call from my cousin, DeeDee. She was also in my bridal party. I had told her that I did not want a Bachelorette Party because I was afraid that my lunatic bridal party girls would bring in a male stripper. She reassured me that it was just going to be a "let's-let-our-hair-down-and-party" type of evening without any guys at all. She was very convincing and I said, *"Oh, what the heck, let's have some fun!"* Poor Michael was probably starting to feel left out; this was already my third all-women, pre-wedding party.

Friday evening "Party Time" arrived, and my bridal party girls, along with some other relatives, were starting to arrive at DeeDee's house. We were all dressed very casually and comfortably in nice jeans and tee shirts. The atmosphere was definitely spicy. My Auntie Mary, who was always very creative, was in charge of the cake, and she made one that entirely resembled the male family jewels. An entire sheet cake size erect penis, along with a pair of testicles, frosted with light flesh tones, and every detail one could imagine, including the medium-brown colored shredded coconut, to resemble pubic hair on the testicles. It was the most outrageous cake we had ever seen. Everything XXX-rated. We were dancing to earsplitting music, and if you wanted a drink there was an overabundance of alcoholic beverages on the counter, chilled with penis-shaped ice cubes... Photos of stark-naked men everywhere, on coasters, walls, glasses and even the usual pin the tail on the donkey this evening would be "pin the penis on the man!" We were hysterical, and they all intended to get me inebriated that evening.

We were having an excessive amount of fun, and I was definitely inebriated. The girls had no problem filling my X-rated glass with as much rum, vodka, whiskey, or whatever they wanted, to the brim. I'm not really much of a drinker, but that night they were going to see to it that I had more alcohol than blood running through my veins. DeeDee decided that she wanted to bring me upstairs to show me something, and like a good pie-eyed drunk, I followed her.

She gently shoved me into the bathroom, and locked me in. Now that was not funny, why was she doing that? I lost my balance and fell into the bathtub. I could hear her laughing hysterically as I was screaming for her to let me out. I had no idea why they were doing this to me, with the exception of perhaps something sneaky happening downstairs.

Finally, she let me out and escorted me downstairs, where an enormous mysterious package wrapped in royal blue foil, and a large white bow was waiting for me. Well, it wasn't a jack in the box, but there was in fact someone in the box. *"Oh, my gosh, I cannot believe it. You guys promised me you wouldn't do this!"*

It was in fact a male stripper. He was a big, brawny dude with dark, olive skin, black wavy hair, beady green paralyzing eyes, and a really prominent nose. He was clad in an abstract necktie hung loosely around his neck and something that resembled a Band-Aid covering his very private parts, which were not so private anymore. I was totally wiped out and angry. I didn't find it too funny at all. They sat me in a chair and he proceeded to do his smutty little dance all around me. Of course, everyone found it quite amusing. I had so much alcohol in me that I don't even think I could feel my own body, let alone feel his.

Everyone was in total pandemonium, enjoying every minute of this, especially when he took off that very tiny patch covering his uncircumcised penis. The alcohol had finally made me lose touch with my senses, and I gave into the overwhelming demand for me to get up, and trip the light fantastic with him. I could not believe that I was dancing with a naked guy! This was most definitely outrageous. So, the party was a big hit, and a most intoxicating time was had by all of us.

8

The week of the wedding had arrived, and Michael and I would soon become husband and wife. All of us involved were trying to tie up loose ends in preparation for the big day, and we were running around like a bunch of lunatics.

My brother had finished his radiation, and even though still very gaunt, his condition was improving and the treatments appeared to have worked. Thank God!

The rehearsal dinner was the night before the wedding at Guido's Italian Restaurant. It was most entertaining, as you can imagine, with twenty-two in our bridal party, not to mention the rest of the friends and relatives that joined us.

The atmosphere was Italian, with soft music playing in the background. The aroma of the food was exquisite. The waiters and waitresses were clad in black slacks, white heavily starched shirts, ruby red neckties, and green aprons.

Everyone was having a good time, and enjoying indulging themselves in the pizzas, with a variety of meats and veggies on top of mounds of steaming deep red sauce and mozzarella. Cheese and spinach-filled ravioli's by the dozen, lasagna several layers thick with cheeses and sauce oozing out of the sides. Lots of meatballs, with that pungent smell of garlic in the air. Fettuccine

Alfredo with an abundance of rich, creamy, white sauce. Tortellinis, rigatonis, manicottis, veal scaloppinis, and Parmesan, all of which were mouthwatering. In addition, if that wasn't enough to whet your appetite, we had dessert, lots of it. Cannolis, rum cakes, custards, biscottis, and last but not least, espresso...that was if the robust, dark, Italian coffee was palatable for you.

We were all having a marvelous time. Well, with the exception of Michael. Although enjoying everything, he seemed really distant that evening. I guessed he just had a lot on his mind. Perhaps, pre-wedding jitters? At the end of the evening, when Michael and I shared a few moments by ourselves, I wondered what was on his mind. The usual glow in his emerald green eyes was not there. Although he was physically holding me, mentally he was not there. Why, I wondered? Had he changed his mind about getting married? His hug was colossal, as if he were never going to see me again. We shared in one last very peppery kiss before going our separate ways for the evening.

The next day we would become husband and wife, and would no longer be going our separate ways. It had seemed like an eternity but we would finally be together as one, to share in the intimacy we had longed for.

That night, my best friend and matron of honor spent the night at my house. It was a long evening; I was quite fidgety, and felt like I had consumed all the espresso, when in fact I hadn't had any. It was just pure adrenaline. At 3:00 a.m., I was still sitting up in bed eating crackers.

Suddenly, Julia sat up, and smacked me across the head; a love tap of sorts, and said, "Now go to sleep!" We were both laughing hysterically. All in all, I think I got two hours sleep, which explained the bags that resembled little pillows above my eyes, and the dark circles like small black tires below them. We were running around like a bunch of confused clowns, trying to prepare for the magical moment that was going to take place in just a few hours.

That morning had been extremely busy for us. I showered, and carefully did my makeup. I wanted everything to look just perfect. Mom took great pleasure in trying to make a bad hairdo not look like a bad hair day. Julia helped me into my wedding dress. Mom and Julia started to cry when they saw me in my lily-white, satin and lace, Southern belle hoop dress, elegantly laced with hundreds of tiny, white pearls, with a lovely satin and lace train, six or seven feet in length, also delicately finished with fine, white pearls. My veil was also lace with pearls, on top of a very exquisite looking hat, which was different from a traditional headpiece.

Our photographer, a long time friend of ours, had arrived, as well as all my beautiful bridesmaids. We were all ready to start our photo session. My mom looked lovely in her pistachio and mint green silk dress. Dad and my brother, Tony, looked very debonair in their black tuxedos. After a couple hours of photos, we were ready to head over to the church.

We loaded up into several beautifully decorated cars, and headed out of our courtyard. Marshall and Edna, our neighbors and good friends, couldn't attend because of an out-of-town guest, but they were there to give us their blessings and watch us drive away. Uncle Nicholas also looked handsome; he was the chauffeur for Dad, Julia, and I. He displayed great pride while driving us in mom and dad's midnight blue Cadillac down the expressway en route to Saint Francis Church.

When we arrived at the church, the parking lot was jam-packed with cars. Our guests were all inside anxiously awaiting our arrival. Everyone including Grandma had already been seated. My mom was still at the rear of the church waiting for my brother to walk her down the aisle. We had hired a singer and a guitar player for our ceremony, and had chosen several songs we wanted them to play. My bridesmaids walked down the aisle to *Sunrise, Sunset*, and my mom and brother to *Evergreen*. I was very touched, to say the least.

Now the only ones left standing, or trembling, in the back of the church were the coordinator, with Dad and I. Dad certainly did look handsome. I knew that he would really have loved to take a few hits on a cigarette. I wondered what he was thinking? The look on his face was pure heaven. The organ music started, and the guests all stood up, and turned to look back at us. At that moment, I think my feet melted right into the floor. My heart was beating like an enormous drum. My adrenaline felt as if it had a turbo boost. My dad took me by the arm with hopes that he could unglue my feet from the floor, and we started to walk down the aisle on the traditional, white carpet runway that was laid down for me.

"This is truly a dream come true. I'm here, it's really happening. Take a deep breath and smile, keep walking... I still cannot believe it's me walking down this aisle! Look at Michael. He looks just as nervous as I am in his dashing black tuxedo with tails, white shirt, black bow tie, and shiny black patent leather shoes. His blonde hair is neatly trimmed, along with his mustache that no longer looks like peach fuzz. His eyes are gleaming and his smile? Well, that says it all..."

We were almost midway down the aisle, and I could see over two hundred smiling faces enjoying every moment of this with wholehearted delight; so much emotion was filling this church. Cameras and video cameras were flashing like lightning, filling the sky from every angle.

Everyone was filled with pure joy. As I got closer to the altar, I could now see clearly how beautiful my entire bridal party looked. It was like walking into heaven. The men all looked so handsome in their black tuxedos, and our ring boy and candle boys wore the same, and looked adorable.

Our bridesmaids in their soft pastel silk dresses, all of which were a different color of the rainbow, with matching floppy brim hats, and color coordinated shoes. Our flower girl was beautiful in her dress which was a replica of mine, with all the white satin, lace, pearls, and hoop; truly a miniature Southern belle doll.

"Who gives this woman to this man?" said Father Bob. Dad said, "I do, Father." The first thing Michael said was, "You look gorgeous." I said, *"Thank you, you look very handsome."* As we held each other's arm, his left with my right, our hearts had already begun to beat with a burning intensity. We walked toward the altar, and Father Bob.

The altar was beautiful, with all the glorious religious figures, including a crucifix of Jesus, on the adjacent wall. There were candles glowing with an eternal light, white roses, carnations, and breathtaking bouquets everywhere.

The ceremony was in full swing, and Father Bob recited some very special prayers. I had something else very special to do that day; I wanted to light a candle at the feet of our beautiful Blessed Mother Statue. Julia very gingerly helped walk me over to the statue, as my train was a mile long.

The church was completely silent. As I made my way over to the statue, I gently lit a candle with a short prayer. I proceeded to turn around and walk back to Michael. Suddenly I saw Julia throw up her arms, and start to run and scream, "Your dress!"

My beautiful, endless train had somehow managed to make it into the candles, and had caught fire. Fortunately, for me, she acted quickly, and put it out before anything serious could happen.

We walked back over to where Michael was; we were now ready to share our wedding vows with each other. As we held each other's warm and sweaty hands, Michael started to share his vows with me. As he pledged his undying love to me, his sparkling, emerald green eyes seemed to once again look right through me.

My heart was beating out of control. My voice crackled as I said, *"I do."* I managed to look deep into Michael's eyes, and it was there that I found his heart. It was now my turn to share my vows with him. I had found the love and passion I knew the two of us were going to share for the rest of our lives. My vows were much like Michael's, the two of us were now as one, and Michael said, "I do."

The two of us then walked over to another very special altar. It was there that we each had one long, white, tapered candle. We joined their flames like our hearts, and lit the one beautiful, white, wedding candle together, becoming one perpetual flame, that of pure love.

Once again we went back to where we recited our vows and where Father Bob said, "You may now kiss the bride." Michael gently raised my veil from my face, and placed it behind me. As we held each other close, our kiss was full of passion. His soft lips felt like heaven, and they were warm and filled with such an intensity that my whole body was ablaze.

Our guests were whistling and applauding as Father Bob proudly announced to all of them, "Ladies and Gentlemen, I now present to you, Mr. and Mrs. Michael Tenaci."

Once again, there were lots of pictures to be taken. Everyone was so exhilarated, and looked so gorgeous. Grandma with her beautiful smile, and soft pink chiffon dress, had such radiance; you could tell it was a very proud moment for her. Grandpa too looked handsome in his light gray, pinstriped suit. My mom in her soft, pistachio green dress looked beautiful, along with my Dad, looking handsome in his black tuxedo. My godparents, brother, and entire bridal party all looked stunning.

9

The temperature was sweltering; almost one hundred degrees. Fortunately, our reception was inside Lou's Village restaurant. The atmosphere was sensational. Our banquet room was elegantly decorated to accommodate our guests, which were in excess of two hundred.

The DJ had already started to play his music, and Michael and I had already shared our first dance as husband and wife. We were having a buffet-style dinner, and everything looked delectable. As with any wedding, the bartenders, host, and hostess were kept busy. We went through countless bottles of beer, champagne, wine, and non-alcoholic beverages.

Michael and I had already felt like we had died and gone to heaven, but the aroma of all this food was piquant. Hot, mouthwatering roast beef, ham, and turkey. Mounds of white fluffy mashed potatoes and gravy. Dinner rolls and steaming hot, fresh veggies, dozens of them. Pans piled high with generous portions of hot, baked lasagna, with layers upon layers of ricotta and other cheeses wedged inside and enveloped with a deep red meat sauce filled with garlic and basil. Colossal meatballs with that pungent aroma of garlic. In addition, if you were not up for the hot stuff and just wanted a simple sandwich, simple is not what you would have found. There were enough cold cuts and cheeses there to feed an army.

Husky-looking potato and macaroni salads. Fruit salads filled with big juicy chunks of sliced apples, oranges, bananas, grapes, and melons, just to name a few. In addition, for those guests that just preferred greens, there were plenty of deep green salads, with all the fixings and a variety of tempting dressings. After eating all of this, I doubted any of us would have room for dessert.

We had the traditional wedding toast, dancing, pictures, and all the lovely things that come with a splendid wedding such as ours. The time went by much too quickly, and soon it was time to cut our wedding cake. It was an exquisite cake, with three different tiers, with a running fountain on the bottom one. There were stairs leading onto smaller side cakes, with little color coordinated figurines resembling our bridal party. It was almost too pretty to cut and eat. Michael and I cut the cake, and he very delicately - as is the tradition - placed a small piece of the delectable, white cake, piled high with fluffy, white, creamy, frosting into my mouth, ensuring he didn't smear what little was left of my makeup, the sweltering heat having taken care of most of it. I, on the other hand was not too gentle in placing a piece of cake into his mouth, which looked oh so inviting, and was compelled to plaster a good part of his heart-shaped lips and rosy cheeks with frosting, little of which made it into his mouth. All of our guests, including ourselves, were really amused by this and what better way to top this off but with a luscious, passion-filled kiss?

Michael and I had the time of our lives at our wedding ceremony and reception. However, it was now time to say goodbye to all of our guests, and get on with our honeymoon. Julia and Jonathan drove us to the airport where we boarded a plane, which would first fly us to Las Vegas, and then in a couple of days on to Los Angeles. Our plane was delayed a bit at the airport so I decided to check in with my family to see how things were coming along. Well, you know us Italians, after the wedding there is always a post-wedding party at our house, with more scrumptious food.

My cousin, Olivia, told me that my parents had been left behind at the reception, and had to have a taxi bring them home. I spoke to my mom, thanked her, told her how much I loved her, but didn't speak with Dad. He was busy having a bit of the bubbly with their guests, and couldn't be found.

I was literally floating on clouds of joy. Michael and I were in flight, and on our way to Las Vegas for our honeymoon. It was a short flight but most enjoyable. We shared several glasses of delectable, Italian sparkling champagne, which were heavenly. By the time we landed in Las Vegas, it was eleven o'clock in the evening. The weather was a sizzling one hundred and seven degrees, and intolerable. Michael didn't waste anytime finding a cab to take us to "Caesar's," the hotel we would be staying in for the next couple of days.

The lights on the Vegas strip were breathtaking; millions of them in every color of the rainbow, flashing brightly to welcome you into the city that never sleeps. My godparents had reserved a beautiful honeymoon suite for us at Caesar's. All eyes were upon us when we arrived, and everyone knew that we were going into the honeymoon suite; it was a bit embarrassing. The bellboy placed our luggage onto a cart, and escorted us to our room. He opened the door for us and this was Michael's cue. He reached over, and gently lifted me up to carry me over the threshold.

The bellboy carefully placed our luggage inside, and without any hesitation quickly exited our room.

This room was unbelievable, and decorated with such elegance. After all, this was "Caesar's Palace." The room was definitely fit for royalty, and for the next couple of days, it would be ours. We had a separate dining area, and enormous his and hers vanity areas. One his and hers shower to share, and the bedroom. *"Oh, my gosh, look at this! Why do they have mirrors on the ceiling above the bed?"* Michael and I walked into the bedroom together to admire what a romantic ambiance it had.

The lights were dim, and we had a rather large, round bed, covered with a soft, ecru colored satin bed spread, delicately trimmed in silk and fine lace, with plump satin pillows on top. Two beautiful crystal glasses, with a fine bottle of chilled champagne on the bedside, were just waiting for us to enjoy, and to top this off, there were mirrors, with gold leaf trim on the ceiling above the bed.

We were both famished, and decided to order an exquisite candlelit dinner for two, right there in our suite. While waiting for our dinner to arrive, we both took refreshing showers before slipping into something "a little more comfortable." I put on a gorgeous white silk negligee, and Michael, well Michael wore boxers and a white tee shirt.

Dinner arrived and the two of us sat at our little antique table enjoying each other's company, drinking our champagne, and savoring our mouthwatering prime rib with horseradish, lobster tail with butter, husky baked potato with a generous portion of butter, sour cream, and chives, fresh veggies, and a crisp spinach salad covered in dressing.

Neither of us ate all that much. Even with the air conditioner on, our room was filled with a feverish kind of heat. The kind of heat caused by two people entirely impassioned. As we finished our glasses of champagne, Michael took me into his arms, and we shared a kiss that was marked with intense emotion. We both had a burning desire to make mad, passionate love; to share the intimacies it seemed we had been waiting an eternity for.

The next morning I was awakened by Michael's voice saying, "Good Morning, Mrs. Tenaci," along with a passionate, yet tender kiss. What a wonderful way to wake up in the morning, snuggled up close to the one you love with such a feeling of euphoria. We had breakfast in bed, which started out with a wholesome glass of orange juice, and a colossal portion of passion.

The next few days were enchanting, and more than anyone could ever dream of. Although Michael and I spent most of our time in our suite, we did our fair share of taking in the sights of the city that never sleeps, before boarding a plane once again, this time en route to Los Angeles.

We took a shuttle to the Disneyland Hotel, where we would be spending the next couple of days. Our suite was romantic, but adorable with the entire Disney decor. It overlooked an enormous pool and Makeshift Island, complete with palm trees and Hawaiian music.

The atmosphere was romantic and full of fun things to do. You don't have to be a child to have fun in Disneyland, Michael and I were like children again. Sitting down at the sidewalk soda shop was a big treat, we ordered a colossal ice cream sundae, with three scoops of creamy, refreshing, French vanilla ice cream, smothered in rich, luscious, chocolate fudge, garnished with fresh, juicy strawberries, mounds of whip cream, sliced almonds, and of course one maraschino cherry to share.

It was as pretty as a picture, but most of all a delectable treat which we enjoyed feeding each other. After spending time on the rides, or with the many adorable characters, we didn't have any trouble creating our own romantic ambiance.

10

All of our wedding gifts were still waiting for us back home, as were our families. We spent time with some of our family and friends, with, of course another scrumptious meal. No matter what the occasion, we eat. It is hard to believe that after all the food we indulge ourselves in; we still stay fit and trim.

Mom and Auntie Ella helped us move several loads of various items to our condo, well, the lightweight things anyway, like the linens and such. Our condo was quaint, with its own pool, and many other amenities. We had plenty of room to chase each other around when the mood suited us.

It was now time to get back in tune with the rest of the world. Technically, we were not still on our honeymoon, but were still enjoying every moment of being newlyweds; it was a sensational feeling that you want to last forever. Like a dream you never want to wake from. Michael was working with my dad and brother, and I was working at home, and couldn't be happier doing all that came with the happy home, including cooking, cleaning, and lovemaking.

Michael and I had a great time decorating our cozy little condominium. Actually it wasn't that little, we had three bedrooms, two bathrooms, a nice family room, and a good sized kitchen where

I would make many scrumptious meals for Michael, myself, and on occasion, for guests. We had lots of closet space, including a vast walk-in closet much like a bedroom in itself, which already had a story to tell. Michael and I could indulge ourselves in passion, no matter where we were in our home. Whether it was hanging up clothes or doing dishes, our time together was precious.

We had been married a couple of weeks, and were still living a fairytale life; married life seemed to be agreeing with us. We were pretty much adjusted to our new home, and every night when Michael came home from work, I would have dinner waiting for him. He had a gigantic appetite, so I always made large portions of everything. My dad always told me that he would rather buy Michael a suit than feed him. I wasn't sure where he put it all with his small body structure.

It was a spaghetti and meatballs kind of day. Michael loved my Italian cooking, so I had prepared my homemade rich, deep red sauce with homemade meatballs and Italian sausage simmering inside it, with a pungent aroma of fresh garlic and basil. I had my spaghetti boiling on the stove, and my green salad completely tossed and in the fridge. As I waited for Michael to come home from work, I helped myself to a slice of hot bread and butter.

I thought about how in love we were. *"Being Michael's wife and lover is very satisfying. There couldn't possibly be anything that could interfere with our happiness. I am deeply in love, I have the man of my dreams who loves me more than life itself, and would do anything for me, for us. Nothing can ever change that."*

Dinner smelt really good, and I couldn't wait for Michael to get home so we could enjoy a nice, quiet dinner and a glass of wine together. The phone rang, and I thought maybe it was Michael, calling to say he would be home late that evening.

11

"Hello...this is Mrs. Tenaci," I said. It was an attorney looking for Michael! What in the world would an attorney want Michael for? *"I'm Michael's wife, can I help you with something?"* The gentleman on the other end of the phone didn't really want to speak with anyone but Michael, and it seemed very confidential. *"You know, considering I'm Michael's wife, you can tell me anything."* I could sense the apprehension in the attorney's voice, which was a bit frightening to me.

The attorney proceeded to tell me that he was representing Michael's girlfriend, and her family. *"What? His girlfriend! You must have the wrong Michael Tenaci! Michael and I were married just two weeks ago, and there is no girlfriend! This has to be a big mistake!"* What the attorney told me next would ultimately crush me.

He said, "I know this is difficult for you to hear, but it's true. Michael has been dating this girl for the past year or so." *"Why does she need an attorney?"* I asked. "Well, Mrs. Tenaci, because she's pregnant with Michael's baby." At that moment, I felt as if all the blood had been drained out of me. The attorney continued to speak to me, but I couldn't move or speak. This had to be a nightmare; it couldn't be true! Not my Michael, he would never do this! He loved me!

I tried desperately to pull myself together; my adrenaline having reached its peak. The attorney explained to me that Michael had to come down to his office to arrange for the baby to be put up for adoption. My legs felt like Jell-O; I couldn't even stand up, and my entire body was trembling. God, please help me with this. *"What do you mean a baby? Michael is going to be a father, and it's not our baby?"*

I felt as if my heart, my whole body, had been crushed. The honeymoon was over, and there wasn't a word in the English dictionary to define what I felt at that moment. After taking down the information, including the girl's name and her parents' phone number, I hung up the phone.

This had to be the most arduous thing I had ever had to endure. I began to pace back and forth in our kitchen, feeling like my entire body was ready to erupt like a fiery volcano. Still alone, I started to scream and cry, talking to myself, and trying to make sense of this nightmare.

This man, the man I fell in love with and married, had a girlfriend? I had to have something to calm me down, I felt like I was losing my mind! *"God, please tell me it isn't so?"*

I ran over to the fridge, grabbed a beer, and without even taking a breath, guzzled it down. I had never even had a sip of beer before that, let alone an entire one. After that, I grabbed another one, opened it, leaned against the kitchen wall, burst into tears, and slowly fell to the floor.

Michael was dating her and having sex with her while we were engaged? How could he have done this to me? Why was this happening? How could he love two people at once? I didn't know where the tears were coming from. Well, yes, I did, they were coming from my broken heart.

Two beers later, and trying to gather my composure, I called Mrs. Doonesbury, the infamous girlfriend's mother. I tried with all my heart to be as congenial as possible, considering the circumstances. I asked, *"What I want to know is, does Michael know any of this? Does he know that he is about to become a father?"*

Mrs. Doonesbury apologized for this unfortunate situation and said, "Yes, he does know about it. His mom told him at your rehearsal dinner." *"What are you telling me? You have got to be kidding? Is she that ruthless? Well, this explains why Michael was so distant at our rehearsal dinner, because his mom had found the kindness in her heart to tell him then that he was going to be a father! Why did she tell him that night? What was her motive?"* Every fiber of my being felt like it had been shredded beyond repair; I was just about ready to take leave of my senses.

I felt no pain, except that of a broken heart. I was so tense and upset that I didn't know what to do. I needed to calm down, and think this through. Divorce seemed like the only logical solution to this. Who the hell was this man that I had fallen in love with?

It was almost five o'clock and dear, sweet, loving Michael was coming through the front door, all smiles. "Honey, I'm home!" My heart felt like it was going to leave my chest. He came into our kitchen and with one steady gaze, looked deep into my eyes, with his emerald green deceiving eyes. He knew something was amiss when he saw me drinking beer.

"Honey, what's wrong?" I said, *"Who do you think you are, calling me Honey? You are nothing but a fucking, lying bastard!"* The look in his eyes told me that he thought he had married a complete nut. Little did he know that what I was about to say had nothing to do with my mental state. He obviously was using the wrong head when he made the choice to sleep with her, while engaged to me.

"Michael, I got a phone call from an attorney looking for you!" Michael's face suddenly took on a very tenebrous appearance. I could almost hear his thoughts, "How does she know?" It was almost as if he could read in my eyes what I was about to tell him. I said, *"Michael, you are about to become a father!"*

He knew exactly what I was saying. He started to cry, and tried to comfort me by saying, "I didn't want you to find out this way!" I said, *"How did you want me to find out, or did you just hope this would go away so that you wouldn't ever have to tell me?"* He continued giving me more excuses than you could imagine, and then said, "Please forgive me, I love you, I only want to be with you!"

I said, *"Michael, I fell in love with you. I thought you were in love with me too. I trusted you with all my heart and now this. Our relationship, our marriage, is one big lie! If you were so in love with me, why did you propose to me when you had another girlfriend? You were uneasy at our wedding rehearsal dinner because your mom had taken the wind out of your sail, and told you that you were going to be a father! Michael, you and I just exchanged our wedding vows. How could you go before God, and look me in the eyes and promise to love me, and to be faithful to me? And what about all those other wonderful things you said that are now just a bunch of lies? Why, Michael? Why did you do this to me? You are a dishonest bastard, and I don't want to have anything to do with you ever again!"*

It seemed as if that argument went on for hours. Finally, I was able to compose myself enough to tell him exactly what the attorney needed him to do; to go to his office, and relinquish all parental rights to his unborn child. The mother, Michael's girlfriend, was going to be sent to Europe to have the baby, and then give it up for adoption. Michael said, "I don't care about the baby, I love you and only you. I will sign whatever papers they want me to. She doesn't mean anything to me, and never did!" How was I supposed to believe a crock such as this?

What was I going to do now? I couldn't tell anyone, with the exception of my best friend, Julia. My family would find this appalling, so I could never tell them. Julia was totally astonished by Michael's behavior, and just kept saying, "I can't believe it!"

As she and I talked, the picture started to become clearer. We looked back on several suspicious situations that just didn't add up at the time. One in particular came to mind, which was our trip to Reno. That evening when I tried to call Michael and the phone rang and rang. Michael claimed that the phone lines must have been down. Yeah, right, the lines were down all right, but they were his lines, and he was so full of shit. There wasn't anything wrong with the lines; he was out all night with his girlfriend!

He was a total jackass, and I fell in love with him! I was the fool that fell for him. His deception had left me wondering how many more surprises he had up his sleeve. How could I make love to him now? Julia thought it would be a good idea to deprive him of his manhood.

Michael and I went to the attorney; it was a very unpleasant situation. Michael couldn't have cared less about his unborn child. He wanted to try and rebuild our relationship; to act as we did before all of this happened. I personally didn't know if that was possible. In my eyes, our engagement, as well as our vows, had been one big fabrication. Well, at least, his vows.

12

I was still in love with him, and couldn't just throw it all away; I couldn't just turn my feelings off, and give up so easily. I must have been crazy, but I decided to give him the benefit of the doubt, and let him prove his love and devotion to me. What I really wanted to do was throw his butt out, but I didn't. This had been a very pebble-strewn beginning to our marriage, and as the days and weeks passed us by, the dreadful memories still clouded my vision of pure love. But, I had decided to be the wife and lover I started out as, in the hopes that perhaps he had learned a valuable lesson from this, and could be the man I thought I fell in love with and married, "For better or for worse."

In every relationship, there are some pebble-strewn paths to walk down, but I had the feeling that with ours, it was going to be more like boulders. I wanted our marriage to work, more than anything in this world. Everything seemed fine; our relationship still seemed to have that burning desire. Our friendship and our passion still flourished.

A late wedding present from Michael was an adorable, coal black, toy poodle. We went together to pick her out; she was the most timid of her litter, her thick, black fur with shiny little curls enveloping her entire little body. As she batted those beautiful, long eyelashes at us, we knew she was the one for us. She was very petite, weighing no more than a pound, and when I picked her up to snuggle her, she warmed up to me, tucking her teeny little body, with ears no bigger than a gumdrop, under my chin.

"Oh, my, there is that puppy breath, she is adorable. I have to have this puppy. Her name will be Bambi." We brought her home to join Bosco, our other adorable, little poodle, named after the chocolate syrup.

As with most of our evenings, love was in the air. However, that night was exceptional; there we were, the two of us together with only the subdued light of the moon, a touch of mood music, and an unbridled sexual desire to appease each other with impassioned, fiery emotions, setting the night on fire. Our hearts beat in unison on a rapturous journey into the still of the night, and its cessation with sleep in each other's arms, only to be awakened with warm, passionate kisses, and the brilliant glow of the morning sun.

Along with all the sensational pleasures in life, come the finances, about which many couples often disagree. Michael and I were sitting at the table one evening paying our monthly bills, which seemed simple enough. I had always thought that Michael might try to take advantage of the fact that my dad was a contractor, with regard to monetary issues. A simple disagreement between us turned into a serious argument.

We had written out our bills, and we now needed to write a check for our life insurance. Michael was making some devious comments, which were very offensive. So I said, *"Michael, you probably married me for money with hopes you could cash in on my life insurance policy someday!"*

Now, the simple bills issue was not so simple. Before I knew it, we were both walking down the hallway, in a very heated exchange of words. Unexpectedly, and without any warning, Michael stopped, turned, and with unbelievable force, belted me across the side of my face. He hit me with such vehement force that I bounced off the wall, and fell to the floor. All I can remember was being very dizzy, and an intense pain on the right side of my face and jaw. Everything seemed cloudy to me; it felt like my brains had been rattled loose. I finally came to my senses, and realized that Michael had, in fact, hit me.

As I lay on the floor crying hysterically, and trying to hold onto what felt like a broken jaw, I was spitting blood out of the sides of my mouth. I couldn't speak. I was not only in shock from taking such a blow to the side of my head, but also that Michael had displayed such a violent outrage. Michael wasn't sure what to do, and I was crying, *"Just go away, look what you did to me!"* Without any hesitation, he left our condo.

I was trembling, and sobbing like a baby. I managed to pick myself off the floor, and get some ice to place on my almost-broken jaw. The inside of my mouth was all torn up from the impact; I was surprised I still had any teeth left. Not only was I hurt physically, but emotionally as well. After our relationship had blossomed into something most couples only dream of, he had to go and hit me! Where did the violent outrage, this hidden temper come from? Who was this man? First, he had a girlfriend while we were engaged, got her pregnant, and now he was abusive too! What was going to happen next? This wasn't a marriage made in heaven. This was a hellish nightmare.

Several hours later, Michael returned home. I was still pretty badly shaken up, and didn't want anything at all to do with him. He tried to apologize and said, "I never wanted to hurt you. I don't know why I did that to you, I'm so sorry, please forgive me?" I was thinking DIVORCE, not forgiveness. It seemed like the only solution to this never-ending nightmare. How many more disappointments were there going to be in this marriage? I didn't even want to think about what he might try next! The Michael I knew was kind, gentle, loving, and very respectful; I wanted that Michael back. I spoke to Julia about this, and she was afraid that Michael might do something like this again, and seriously hurt me. I told her that I would be careful and pay close attention to his behavior.

13

It was already December 1981, and winter was upon us. There hadn't been any more surprises with regard to Michael, in the past several months, we seemed to have rebuilt our little love nest and it was stronger than ever. However, something was wrong, and I wasn't feeling well at all. I was extremely nauseous and every time we kissed I got sick from the smell of his mustache wax; it was repulsive. This had never happened to me before, and was very extraordinary. Maybe I had the flu? If I didn't feel any better in the next couple of days, I would have to call my doctor.

It was almost five o'clock, and Michael would be home from work soon. I had our dinner baking in the oven. *"I must have the flu, nothing smells or taste good, and I feel so unhealthy. I hope I am able to enjoy this dinner with Michael tonight,"* I thought.

On any other day, the aroma of my dinner would have been mouthwatering. However, that night, once again, I couldn't even stand being in the kitchen; I was going to have to excuse myself from dinner that evening. *"Is this sleep deprivation? I am so tired and depleted of energy."* Well, maybe I could try a little bit of dinner; perhaps it would help settle my stomach.

The special in the Tenaci kitchen that night was a plump, juicy, baked chicken, smothered in a dark, robust sauce, seasoned with an abundance of fresh pungent cloves of garlic, and enormous fresh, deep green, sweet basil leaves from the garden, along with other family secrets. Potatoes, lots of potatoes, cut into quarters, and immersed under the delectable sauce, along with diced onions, strong enough to bring tears to your eyes, and carrots, sliced to perfection. Fluffy, long grain white rice, piled high like Pikes Peak, and piping hot French bread with a heavenly scent. Michael loved to dip the hot bread into the sauce.

As we sat down to eat dinner, it had become apparent to me that I was really sick, and there was no way that I could even sit in the kitchen, let alone consider eating dinner; I felt like I was going to lose the contents of my stomach. Michael, on the other hand could eat dinner, no matter what. Suddenly a little light went off inside my head. Let's see now; I have been excessively nauseous, every smell or fragrance makes me feel ill, and falling asleep just around six o'clock in the evening sounds a bit curious. Well, I was late for my period. Was it possible that I was pregnant?

After Michael had finished his dinner, he could see that I was not feeling well and had lain down on the sofa. So, he took it upon himself to clean up the kitchen for me. Even though I liked to do my own domestic duties, he was good about helping out. Sometimes these little chores turned into romantic interludes but not that night. We did snuggle up next to each other on the sofa, although not until Michael had gone in and washed off the remnants of his mustache wax;

the smell was causing something fierce to happen in my stomach.

Later that evening, Michael and I discussed the possibility that I might be pregnant, which would have made us both very happy. He decided it was time to take a little trip down to our neighborhood pharmacy to pick up one of those home pregnancy kits. The instructions looked simple enough. A bit of urine on this strange little contraption, and let it sit for twenty minutes. No color, you're not pregnant and if it turns blue, you are! Michael and I cuddled on the sofa again, waiting not-so-patiently for the results; twenty minutes seemed like an eternity that evening, as we waited to find out whether we were about to become parents.

14

We were about to become proud parents, and were overjoyed with the news. This was truly a miracle for both of us. How could there be anything more exhilarating in one's life than to find out you are to become a Mommy or a Daddy? We couldn't wait to share this wonderful, exciting news with everyone.

When we made our surprise announcement, our family and friends, especially my parents, were elated. After all, they were about to become grandparents for the first time, having waited patiently to hear this wonderful news. My brother was just about ready to break out the "I'm a proud Uncle" cigars.

The morning sickness was unbearable; every day for a couple of months I felt as if I had a fatal flu bug, accompanied by a bad hangover. Even though I was very sick, Michael and I were amazed at my appetite, which seemed to be unending; if I didn't eat, I got more nauseous. I couldn't tolerate the smell of chicken at all.

My favorite food was artichokes, stuffed Italian style with lots of garlic, Romano cheese, parsley, breadcrumbs, olive oil, salt, pepper, and then steamed to perfection. I could eat several at one sitting.

Once past the morning sickness stage, everyone began to spoil me rotten. My family and friends were in their element watching my tummy grow to gigantic proportions; my clothes were starting to look like they would be fit for an elephant. My petite little body had gone from the "big" maternity clothes to the "jumbos," and Michael was gaining weight right along with me. He had put on a good twenty pounds or so.

Italian, Mexican, Chinese, or American, it didn't matter what type of cuisine it was; I had an insatiable appetite. Ice cream, lots of ice cream. I especially craved green tea ice cream, which is extremely bland, and yet tasted so delicious. My Dad and brother drove all over town looking for it, and bought a gallon for me.

My cravings did not seem to have a specific pattern, at all hours of the night, I woke up with an appetite for the most unusual foods, and Michael was always more than happy to accommodate me. The two of us often sat in bed in the wee hours of the morning snacking on one thing or another. He found it all very amusing.

It seemed so funny that, even when pregnant, with my body growing to gigantic proportions, Michael still loved me, actually seemed to love me more. Was it because I was carrying our child? What is it about being pregnant that your significant other finds so attractive? Maybe it was the new and improved breast size, which had gone from 32B fried eggs to a colossal 36D watermelons? Whatever it was, it was heavenly.

Michael and I spent hours cuddling. It was fascinating to watch our baby kicking and moving all around inside my tummy. Michael enjoyed massaging my tummy, and at the same time being able to feel our baby growing inside; even though my body was quite large, we were still caught up in the moment enjoying the intimacies the two of us shared. Considering the condition of my body, our passionate moments were a bit more delicate or tranquil in nature, but still very fulfilling.

Everyone wondered whether our new little "Baby Tenaci" was a bouncing baby boy or girl; there was lots of guessing going on. Auntie Ella seemed to be the most accurate with all pregnancies; she had it down to a science, and thought our baby was going to be a little girl. I thought so too. It didn't matter to Michael and I whether it was a girl or a boy; either one was a blessing.

I was in the last trimester of my pregnancy, and pleasingly plump. Once again, my family had outdone themselves and given me a surprise baby shower with lots of family and friends, most of whom I hadn't seen since our wedding. We had an Italian-style buffet luncheon.

My Mom, Grandma, aunties, and cousins all made some delectable treats. I could see Grandma's famous homemade pizzas, still piping hot and fresh from the oven, smothered in a delicious red sauce, with mozzarella, chunks of Italian sausage, anchovies, mushrooms, green onions, garlic, and olives, piled high on the golden mouthwatering crust, cut into generous portions.

Large pans full of chunky baked lasagna with layer upon layer of thick pasta, ricotta, and other cheeses smothered in a delectable meat sauce. Hot, homemade breads, mounds of scrumptious chunky potato, macaroni, and fruit salads. Spicy gourmet hot peppers, pickles, and olives grown right there in Mom and Dad's backyard.

Juicy and tender roast beef, ham, turkey, salami, and a variety of Italian and American cheeses. Do I dare mention the desserts? The cake was gigantic and truly adorable; a white chiffon cake filled with thick, creamy custard, and topped with an abundance of silky, whipped cream laced with soft baby pastel rose buds. Grandma's special brightly colored rainbow Jell-O blended with whipped cream and secret fruit juices, set inside a delicious ladyfinger mold. And let's not forget the beverages; there seemed to be a river of beverages of all sorts flowing from the fountain.

Baby showers are so much fun; we women really know how to have a good time at a shower. Everything was absolutely wonderful, and everyone was so amused by my enormous size. After all, most of them hadn't seen me since the wedding, and no I didn't think my wholesome, plump body could still fit into that sexy, black teddy from "Victoria's Secret."

"Look at all of these adorable little outfits, and all the lovely things that our baby will use in his or her nursery. There is at least one of everything that I could ever possibly need. Handmade blankets crocheted with soft baby blues, pinks, buttercup yellows, mint greens, and snowy whites. Pajamas, many tiny little pajamas with booties, tee shirts, and what looks like an entire new wardrobe; baby already has more clothes than we do. A beautiful maple crib with dresser, stroller, car seat, playpen and countless other adorable gifts. This is heavenly and more than anyone's heart could desire."

15

Being pregnant in late August was very uncomfortable; the sun was blazing hot with temperatures sizzling into the triple digits, and considering I had gained at least forty pounds or so, it was really becoming arduous for me to walk, sit, or even breathe. All of the extra weight, and pressure from the baby had caused me to get those awful little things that resemble grapes coming out of my bottom; just what I needed, a dangling participle.

Michael and I had been attending Lamaze classes, which all of us expectant mommies and daddies know should be taken seriously. Our instructor was very compassionate, with a superlative sense of humor, and tried to make sure we were all comfortable with what we were learning. *"This is just what we all needed to add to our new and improved waistlines, milk and cookies..."*

I was ten days late, and thinking to myself that it was enough already. This couldn't be happening to me; I knew that we calculated the due date correctly. Every day that went by, we all grew more excited and impatient. If our family statistics, or the science my godmother used was as accurate as it had been in the past, our little bundle of joy would be a baby girl. We had tried everything to bring on my labor; even something from an old wives' tale; a teaspoon of castor oil, which is quite revolting. It was like swallowing motor oil. That didn't work either.

Someone suggested that maybe a passionate moment or two would help speed things along? I hardly felt voluptuous, with my tummy the size of a wine barrel, my breasts feeling like they were going to explode, and a bottom that's dam was going to break lose at any time.

These old wives tales left much to be desired. Then, I had a sudden burst of energy and while sitting down, I did a little bit of ironing. Everyone says that you get a burst of energy when you are about to go into labor. *"This is probably just another one of those old wives' tales."*

"I wonder why my tummy feels like it is being pulled taut from all angles? Why is it making such an unusual shape? And why is it taking my breath away? I have never had this feeling before..." Trickle, trickle...water slowly started to seep out, and down my legs.

My heart was racing expeditiously; I was excited, nervous, and frightened all at the same time. *"Michael, I think my water just broke!"* Michael was in a bit of a panic, his eyes were as big as saucers, and the color of his skin had suddenly turned bone white. *"Michael? I think it's time!"*

Michael and I arrived at the hospital with your typical craze for first time parents; the contractions were ten minutes apart and very intense. Mom, Dad, Tony, Julia, and DeeDee just about beat us to the hospital.

Broom Hilda, I mean the nurse, handed me a lovely, white flowing gown; the kind that allows your buttocks to hang out. *"These are definitely not from Victoria's Secret Fall Designs."* My contractions were already so intense that I didn't really care what part of me was showing. Even though the nurse didn't fly in on her broom this time, to me, she was still a witch. After my first exam, she called my doctor and conveyed to him that my water hadn't broken yet, and so I was sent back home.

"What is wrong with these doctors and witches (I mean nurses)? I'm in labor, and they are sending me home?" Michael and I went on home, and so did the rest of our family and friends. Michael climbed back into bed and within seconds, it seemed, was snoring; he could sleep through a nuclear attack. I was very uncomfortable, sitting on the side of our bed, and at a snail's pace, lifting one leg at a time and trying to get my pleasingly plump little body onto our bed. As I lay down, my tears were overflowing down my pie-shaped face, and onto my fluffy, goose down pillow. The contractions were still very intense, and now five minutes apart.

I was trying to remember the Lamaze breathing, but I was in so much pain that I couldn't concentrate on them. *"Michael, please take me back to the hospital, I'm in labor and this is really painful."*

Michael finally awoke from the grave (it seemed), helped me roll off our bed, and walked me with prudence back outside to the car. The more I cried, the snappier his driving became.

The witch must have fallen into her own brew; the night shift was now on, and I had an angel for a nurse this time. *"Thank you, God."* My contractions were very unpleasant and this time I was not going home. *"Well, at least not until I have my baby."* I had back labor; the most dreaded labor of all, and it was intolerable.

Michael tried to help with my breathing but it seemed hopeless. So DeeDee took over as breathing coach, while Michael and Tony pressed on my lower back and hips during the contractions to help ease the excruciating pain; the immense pressure they were applying was an attempt to counteract the unbearable pressure I was feeling from the inside.

Several hours had passed, and the pain was so intense that I felt I had taken leave of my senses; I was delirious and screaming out of control. *"Something is wrong, I can't take this anymore. Please help me!"* Finally, my doctor reexamined me, only to find that my water had, in fact, broken; the witch had made a big booboo. I had no water left inside of my pelvis, and it was going to be a dry birth. Although I was still dilating very slowly, my contractions were off the chart, but my doctor still believed in all-natural childbirth.

No breathing techniques in the world were going to help me. *"I just have to scream!"* The pain was so intense that I ripped Michael's shirt. Twenty-six hours into labor and still only eight centimeters dilated; still two more centimeters before I could deliver.

My doctor, nurse, and coaches now had me biting on towels to keep me from bearing down. If I bear down or push too soon, my cervix would swell, and I wouldn't be able to deliver vaginally. *"I can't do this, it hurts too much!"*

My body was floundering violently from side to side, and I continued to cry out in earsplitting screams. I was out of control. *"Somebody please help me, I can't do this! This isn't childbirth, this is torture!"*

By now, I had scared the life out of all my family and friends. They had been sent into the lobby, and because of my intense screaming my doctor had closed off my room, with the exception of my coaches.

"Ten, I'm dilated to ten! Oh, thank you, dear Lord. Please, help me deliver my baby, please stop the pain, I can't take it anymore!" I was terrified, and felt like I had lost my marbles; they placed me onto the delivery bed, and into the stirrups of the Wild West, *"Yee Haw!"*

There we go, a little, well not so little, injection for the episiotomy, and a lot more screaming. *"Oh my God, what is he going to do with those?"* Because it was a dry birth, a forceps delivery was unavoidable. *"Those things look like giant salad tongs, you can't use those on me!"*

We were now into the twenty-seventh hour of intense labor. Push, Push, Push. Baby coming through my birth canal facing the wrong direction. Forceps... and one long, intense blood curdling screammmmmm!

16

On September 2, 1982, at eleven thirty eight p.m., a voice, that of an angel, could be heard crying out at the foot of the bed; it was the voice of our baby girl announcing to the world that she had indeed arrived. She was seven pounds, four and a half ounces of pure joy. I was totally overcome with emotion, and my tears were not from the pain, but from the happiness in my heart. Michael was thrilled, and I think, in shock. DeeDee was crying right along with us, and couldn't get enough of snapping all the Kodak moments possible.

There were no words to express my feelings when I held her in my arms for the first time, and kissed her smooth, rosy cheeks; I couldn't believe that I was holding my daughter in my arms. She already knew whom I was, who had given her life, and with this, our bonding had begun. With her little head snuggled up under my chin, I felt like I was melting.

We named her Millie and she was so precious, with a perfectly round little head, thick, black wavy hair, lots of it, resembling that of an Eskimo, an olive complexion with chunky, rosy cheeks, big light-colored eyes, a tiny little pug nose, and tiny pink heart-shaped lips. You could tell that I fed her well because she was quite the little chunkster. She had rolls upon rolls; her little arms and legs looked like we pumped them up, and her skin was smooth and delicate. Ten tiny little fingers and toes with dainty snow white nails. Just perfect, everything was perfect.

I gently handed her to Michael so that he could cuddle our new little daughter; he was overwhelmed, and couldn't take his eyes off her, holding her as if she were a fragile piece of glass that would break. As she lay all snuggled up in her soft, pink blanket in his arms, he kissed her tenderly on her plump, rosy cheeks.

Now it was DeeDee's turn. We called her the hog; whenever there was a baby around, she wanted it all to herself. She was all wrapped around Millie, laughing and crying at the same time. I don't know what I would have done, had Michael, DeeDee, and my brother not been there to coach me.

As Michael very gingerly walked Millie down the hallway into the nursery, she had quite the welcoming party waiting to catch a glimpse of her. Aunts, uncles, godparents, grandparents, cousins, and friends... it looked like a wedding reception there in the hallway of the nursery. After such an outrageously stressful twenty-seven hours of intense labor, our family and friends were overwhelmingly exhilarated. I was sure that they were all suffering from sleep deprivation, and would welcome a good night's sleep.

Dr. Bob did have some concerns about Millie's health because she was a dry birth, and unfortunately because she had swallowed some fluids that were not healthy for her. She would be monitored closely before being sent home. She seemed to be thriving, but I knew that she was waiting patiently for my milk to come in.

"Lord, have mercy, what an awful feeling! My breasts feel like they are going to explode with all the milk in them. I guess this is what Millie was waiting for. My breasts feel like they are exploding, my buttocks has been sewn beyond hope, and my back and hips are knocked out of whack from the labor and coaches pushing on them. I need to get this old body in shape so that I can take care of my precious, new arrival."

I was in seventh heaven, and really couldn't believe that I was a Mommy, holding my beautiful, little baby. This was incomparable to anything I had ever experienced. Her smile, her cry, the way she snuggled up to me, and the clean fresh baby scent that was dreamy... I just wanted to hold her forever.

She truly was a miracle, a precious gift. Grandma and Grandpa, the very proud grandparents, were waiting patiently at our condominium for Millie's arrival, and their chance to cuddle their first grandchild. We were making another memory; there wasn't anything in the world that could make them any happier than holding their grandchild for the first time. Uncle Tony was also there, holding Millie as if she were fragile crystal. You could see the pure joy in his eyes, and how proud he was to be an uncle. They were all going to spoil Millie rotten!

Michael and I were truly enjoying every day with Millie; sharing in the responsibilities a newborn brings, with the exception of breastfeeding, which was my department. Diaper duty, however, was definitely shared. We enjoyed putting Millie in bed with us in the mornings, and snuggling with her; she looked so tiny lying on our big bed, loving every moment of it. It was so much fun to dress her up every day. Her wardrobe looked like a children's boutique.

The first year seemed to fly by, full of wonderful firsts including Baptism, Thanksgiving, Christmas, New Year, Easter and, of course, teething, crawling, that first step, first words, the big first birthday, and the list goes on and on.

Our lives were so full with Millie; she was so good-natured, and quite the character. Her favorite toys were not made of plastic; they were our poodles, Bosco and Bambi. She was crazy about them. I don't think she realized they were not toys.

Julia called me one morning, as her grandmother was in town from Canada, and they wanted to come by and see Millie, so I invited them over for coffee and cake. Grandma J. fell in love with Millie, who was a typical little clown when we had company.

While Millie was entertaining our guest, Julia and I were in the kitchen cleaning up. As we were standing at the sink, dear, sweet Michael strolled in, and pinched Julia on the butt! *"Oh, my God! I can't believe what just happened here! Did she really allow him to do that, and is she as shocked as I am? What is his problem? This is my best friend that he just pinched, and I am his wife! I feel like a firecracker ready to detonate."*

Neither of us had words. For a moment, the world seemed to have stopped turning. It came so naturally, almost as if it were not the first time he had done it, and it was all too comfortable for him. Maybe that awful feeling I had had in my gut about him having a thing for her was not just a feeling? Every time he saw her, he gave her a kiss on the lips. He was always so excessively enthusiastic and wild-eyed. This had to be one-sided. There was no way that she would ever do anything like that to me with my husband. I thought Michael had some serious issues. I could hardly wait to get out of the kitchen, and my blood was boiling over. I had to excuse myself, and go into the bathroom. My body was trembling. Had this man no gumption? He was just full of surprises!

I called Michael into the back bathroom, and he acted as if nothing had happened, a real saint. I was sure he could see the blaze of fire in my eyes, hear the thunder in my voice, and knew that I was near frothing. "What did I do now?" he said. *"Michael, you know what you did now!"* I replied. *"I *thought you had learned a lesson way back in the beginning of our marriage? What the hell do you think you are doing pinching Julia's butt?"* "I didn't pinch her butt, you don't know what you are talking about!" he said, getting all flustered, and denying the entire situation. *"I can't believe you can stand here, look me straight in the eyes, and deny this?"* I said. He said, "Give me a break, why would I do that with you standing there?" *"Hmmm, does that mean he does it when I'm not around?"*

As I took deep breaths to try to calm my now sizzling body, Michael walked out of the bathroom. I wondered what Julia was thinking. I was sure she knew why I called him down the hall; he had really put us all in an awkward situation. Well, I couldn't stay in the bathroom all night. After all, we did have guests. So, I went back down the hall to try to be a good little hostess, and act like nothing had happened. The air was so thick you could cut it with a knife. Michael was acting as if he had a giant gas bubble. I was starting to feel like my marriage was more like "Mr. Toad's Wild Ride!"

It was already 1984, and we had just purchased and moved into our first home. Millie was one and a half by then, and quite the little character with her tenacious personality. She had a petite, little body, shoulder length, golden-brown, wavy hair, a face as round as an apple pie, big brown eyes, and a smile that could light up the sky.

She was really enjoying our enormous backyard, which was designed with all that a small child's heart could desire. She had a gym dandy swing set, with a slide into a colossal sand box loaded with toys. We had a large patio where she could play mini-basketball, ride her little bicycle, roller skates, or even her power wheels motorized cycle.

She had a playhouse with dolls, and all that you could imagine. Michael and I often set aside being adults, and played with her in the backyard; the three of us always had so much fun together, swinging, building sand castles and even looking like a circus act, riding her tiny little bikes with her.

The only thing missing in this picture was a sibling. Millie would have loved a little brother or sister. Michael and I sure had fun trying, but we hadn't been successful yet. Millie was the joy of our lives, and we wanted another child just as precious as she was; we knew she would make such a wonderful big sister.

One morning, I woke up feeling exhausted, not wanting to get out of bed. However, even if you do feel like death warmed up, when you have a small child, you can't just stay in bed. *"I can just imagine a toddler, my inquisitive little Millie, without any supervision in our house. I need to drag myself out of bed, like right now. I'm so nauseous though. I think maybe the fast food we had last night must have given me food poisoning. I wonder how Michael is feeling at work today? Millie seems to be just fine."* I called Michael, and he was just fine. *"Well, both Millie and Michael are fine, what is my problem? Wake up, Mommy, and smell the coffee! Maybe I'm pregnant? We have been trying, and this would be such wonderful news!"*

Millie and I took a trip to the pharmacy to pick up a pregnancy test. She was still much too young to really understand what a pregnancy test was. *"If it's positive, I will explain to her that we are going to have another little baby, and she is going to have a baby brother or sister. She will be so excited and Michael is going to be so happy, because we have wanted another baby for such a long time."* Millie and I purchased the pregnancy test, and a little book. She liked her little storybooks, and every time we went to the store, we bought her one. We stopped for some lunch, and then went home.

17

"Look, Millie, it's blue! We are going to have another baby!" The pregnancy test did in fact confirm a pregnancy. The two of us sat on the sofa with her little book, which just so happened to talk about baby brothers and sisters. I was not going to tell her that a stork was going to bring us a baby; I told her that Mommy had a baby growing in her tummy, of course with cautious details. All she needed to know was that we were going to have another baby, and she didn't really care if it was the stork, Santa Claus, or magic that brought it; she was just so excited that she would soon have a little playmate. *"Well, at least now I know that I don't have food poisoning. Michael is going to be delighted."*

"Honey, Millie, I'm home!" Yes, that would be Michael, with his usual greeting when he came home from work. Millie loved her daddy, when daddy came home from work, she stopped whatever she was doing, and ran to get her big teddy bear hugs and kisses. The sun rose and set with daddy. Millie and I were very close, beyond words; however, there is something about little girls and their daddies...

So, Michael wanted to know how I was feeling, and Millie felt obliged to tell him that we were going to have another baby! He was thrilled with the good news. This meant that the three of us would soon become four.

Michael, Millie, and I carried on with life as usual. I had a small balloon business that I ran from home, and Millie and I usually kept busy with that; she thought she was the boss, and had a great time with all the balloons.

My waistline was starting to grow, and it was becoming obvious that we were expecting again; it was so exciting. For some reason though, the morning sickness, breast tenderness, and all that comes with being pregnant, including increased appetite, had disappeared. I was concerned because my doctor said that all these symptoms are good signs of a strong pregnancy. *"What is wrong with my pregnancy? Why do I suddenly not feel pregnant?"*

I had become very troubled by this feeling, or rather not feeling, and decided that I should follow up with my obstetrician. Therefore, I dropped Millie off at Grandma and Grandpa's, and headed for my doctor's appointment.

My doctor couldn't hear the baby's heartbeat, which was distressing news. I said, *"This can't be happening. There has to be some mistake. Maybe the reason you can't hear the heartbeat is how the baby is turned?"* My doctor was speaking softly, trying not to alarm me too much, but I could see the disquietude in his face, which didn't make me feel too comfortable. He wasn't sure, so just to be on the safe side, he sent me for an ultrasound.

SARA TENACI
THAT'S ANOTHER CUP OF COFFEE

18

At the ultrasound, I was so excited to see my tiny little baby on the screen. The baby seemed to be doing just fine, however, the news was not good. With a very somber look on her face, the doctor revealed to me that my baby's heartbeat had stopped, and that this was a non-viable pregnancy. I said, *"Does this mean that my baby has died?"*

She said, "Yes, I'm sorry, it appears that the fetus has no heartbeat." My eyes started to well up, and the tears flowed endlessly down my cheeks. *"Oh, my God, why my baby? What am I going to tell Michael and Millie? They are going to be so heartbroken."*

The doctor told me that my body would spontaneously abort the baby, which meant that I had to carry on like a normal person. I had a baby inside me that had died, and they wanted me to carry on as if nothing was wrong?

Over the next few weeks I became very disturbed and uneasy. My baby was still in my tummy, not living, and for some reason was not coming out on its own. I didn't want all of this to have a negative effect on Millie, and tried desperately to put it in the back of my mind, and not dwell on it, but she wanted to know why Mommy was so sad and crying all the time. After weeks of heartbreak and unrest with this, my doctors had to go in surgically, and remove the baby from my uterus, reassuring us that we should be able to have another healthy pregnancy.

Michael, Millie, and I are carried on with our lives, and even though having a miscarriage was heartbreaking, we tried not to let it consume us. We had been blessed with Millie, she was truly wonderful, and nothing could ever change that.

She was growing up right before our eyes, and turning into quite the little professor. Since she didn't have siblings around, we put her into Challenger preschool to be with other kids her own age.

She was learning to be a child, enjoying all that comes with childhood, instead of the adult she thought she was. She loved her teachers, Ms. Carol and Ms. Mona, and they were wonderful with her.

Time was passing by so quickly, and it appeared that Millie was going to be an only child; she often asked why we couldn't have another baby for her. Over the years, we had tried and tried to give Millie a little brother or sister. *"I guess it is just not meant to be."* I had endured surgery, and six heart-wrenching miscarriages; an emotional roller coaster. My doctor was puzzled, but still insisted that this was just a statistic. Each miscarriage took so much out of me, out of all of us. It was mentally, physically, and emotionally draining. Should we just stop trying, and let Millie be an only child? Should we adopt? I had been pregnant seven times, and had one precious little girl. Was there a message in this? *"Michael, maybe it is time now to move on, and not worry about any more pregnancies. We have Millie, and she is our blessing. This has consumed me!"* Michael said he would support whatever my decision was on this, and that he would love Millie and me no matter what I decided.

19

"If I didn't know any better, I would say this is morning sickness. I don't know what has come over me." I had flu-like symptoms, motion sickness even while standing or sitting still, cravings, very unusual cravings, and breast tenderness, but sometimes the mind can play funny tricks on us. After wanting so much to become pregnant and have another baby, maybe I was having a false pregnancy? I hadn't paid too much attention to the due date of my period, so it was possible I was late.

Ten days late to be exact, and a trip to the obstetrician for a pregnancy test confirmed that I was pregnant for the eighth time. *"How did this happen? I mean, I know how it happened, but..."*

Michael, Millie, and I were so excited, but very apprehensive about the news. This time, my doctor gave me some specific progesterone hormones, specially prepared by the pharmacist. My body would absorb only what it needed to maintain the pregnancy; apparently, a lack of hormones was causing my miscarriages.

Morning sickness, good appetite, breast tenderness, and all those feelings you normally dread during pregnancy, were a welcome feeling to me. They were all signs that showed my pregnancy of three months was a strong one.

Since all my miscarriages had been at three months, this was a critical period for me.

I thought a little trip down south to that "Happiest Place on Earth" called Disneyland would be fun for Millie's fourth birthday. Michael, Grandma, Millie, and I decided the weather was really beautiful at that time of year, and we should drive down instead of flying. The long drive didn't seem to bother my tummy all that much and it didn't really matter to me, as long as my hormones were strong enough to hold this pregnancy. Millie was so anxious; I don't think she stopped talking for seven hours straight in the car.

Arriving at the Disneyland Hotel was a welcome sight, especially after having driven for seven hours. Seeing Millie's big, sparkling brown eyes, and bright smile, and hearing the excitement in her voice was in itself magical and well worth any drive to get there. As we walked through the entry gates, we were greeted by those two famous mice, Mickey and Minnie, clad in their bright red, white, and black outfits, with a hint of yellow trim.

It didn't take Millie long before she warmed right up to them, and all the other characters in the Hometown Square; she was getting plenty of autographs as well. She also took it upon herself to go into the character's dressing room, and came out holding hands with Goofy! It was heartwarming, and one of the cutest and funniest things I have ever seen. As she raced around speaking with all the characters, it was obvious that her adrenaline had reached an all-time high.

Michael, Grandma, and I just sat back and enjoyed watching this precious little girl, our little girl, with long, golden-brown, wavy hair past her bottom, big, brown eyes, and a smile that would light up the sky, having the time of her life.

Grandma was delighted to watch her granddaughter have so much fun, and Michael and I, well, we had that warm, fuzzy feeling. Being here together creating memories with Millie was pure fantasy.

In addition, for Michael and I, the last time we were in the place where dreams come true, Disneyland, was on our honeymoon. Who would have ever thought that several years later we would be sitting on that same bench, watching our own little girl creating memories?

Millie was overwhelmed with all the enormous, brightly colored rides with variations of character themes. Her favorite ride was the Matterhorn; amazing that a child of only four years old loved that ride, with its lightening-quick cars, weaving in and out of all the tunnels of the simulation of the Pennine Alps, bordering Switzerland and Italy. It took my breath away, but she wanted to ride it repeatedly. I was surprised that in my pregnant condition the attendants even let me on the ride; I guess they didn't realize I was pregnant, and perhaps just thought I had indulged myself in one too many hamburgers!

During our three-day stay in Disneyland, we went on every ride possible, saw all the shows, characters, and parades, and satisfied ourselves with all sorts of delectable goodies. Our little baby growing in my tummy had been to Disneyland, and didn't even know it yet.

We arrived back home on Sunday evening, having all had a wonderful time in Disneyland, especially Millie. If it was up to her, she would have adopted some of the characters, and brought them home with us. Instead, she compromised by coming home with bags of souvenirs in all shapes and sizes. Grandma also had a great time but was happy to be back home with Grandpa.

I had passed the critical third month, as well as the fourth month of my pregnancy, and we couldn't have been more pleased. Michael was working everyday, while I was the domestic engineer, but most importantly the mommy, and enjoying every minute of my time with Millie. We had just purchased a brand new home; three bedrooms, two bathrooms, in a court with a large lot, and plenty of room for our children to play and have fun. I made sure that Millie was included in all the planning and decorating for our house, as well as for her little baby brother or sister due to make an appearance in a few months time.

"I know that I'm not lifting anything that I'm not supposed to, so why am I am having these cramps and why am I spotting? Oh, my God, I can't be losing this baby too! I'm over the critical stage, this can't be happening to me again!" Michael was always at work when there was a crisis, so this time Millie and I went to the doctor's office to see why I had started to have cramps, accompanied by spotting. The doctor said, "The only thing we can do is to increase the hormones and hope that will work. Apart from that, there isn't a whole lot more we can do."

So, there I was at almost the halfway point in my pregnancy, and my body was threatening to miscarry... *"I can feel my baby's movement in my tummy, and my doctor let me hear the heartbeat, it's still strong... all we can do is pray."* The next forty-eight hours were going to be touch and go; I hoped that the hormones would be absorbed fast enough to make a difference. *"I just can't bear the thought of losing another baby now; especially after all I have already been through."*

20

Once again we had made it past another critical stage in my pregnancy; the increased hormones seemed to be what my body needed. *"I think that I am going to be on pins and needles my entire pregnancy."* We tried to put this incident behind us, and look forward to the holidays, which were right around the corner.

It was Christmas 1986, and this would be our first Christmas in our new home. Millie was so excited that Santa would be coming soon; that year she had asked him for a swing set. She was quite an inquisitive little girl, trying to figure out how Santa was going to bring a swing set down the chimney. *"Well, you know that magical stardust helps him bring all the toys down the chimney."*

Millie really enjoyed decorating our beautiful, dark green, ten-foot tall, white fur Christmas tree; Christmas was definitely in the air with the Chipmunks singing Christmas carols, and the bright glow of the fire crackling and warming our very festive family room.

Michael, Millie, and I strung literally thousands of tiny bright rainbow-colored little twinkle lights in and out of every branch, and all the way around, making sure not to miss a spot. *"This has to be perfect for Santa!"* We had a nice collection of ornaments, and Millie thoroughly enjoyed placing them on the tree, in the most gingerly fashion, which was just adorable.

It was Christmas Eve, and traditionally we spent most of it at my parents' house with my brother, Michael's family, and great Grandma Chirco. My Mom and Grandma are by far the two best Italian cooks around. We were at Grandma and Grandpa's place, the one where they had given their grandchildren lots of love, and spoilt them rotten. So far, though, Millie was still the only grandchild, with another one on the way. It seemed that all we were going to do that day was eat, and open presents.

The spread was very Italian, with lots of delectable foods, including fresh, cracked crabs boiled right in our kitchen, marinated in special Italian juices including extra virgin olive oil, lots of pungent cloves of fresh garlic, oregano, and some other secrets that just make your mouth water, especially when you dunk your homemade, fresh-from-the-oven, golden-brown, Italian, sourdough bread into the tasty juices. Then we had piles of fried calamari seasoned to perfection, breaded and deep-fried golden brown, crunchy smelt, dozens of colossal steamed prawns sautéed in our secret olive oil, garlic, and a little bit of this and that, to really make your saliva glands do the dance of delectation. Husky well-seasoned and batter-fried cauldoni, cut into generous portions, which look like celery and are from the artichoke family; you can't stop eating these until the plate is emptied. There were also lots of appetizers, wines, beers, sodas, coffee, biscottis. Our menu was immeasurable.

Let's not forget the delicious pasta with meatless sauce, and an abundance of pungent garlic, smothered in a sharp pecorino cheese. One of our Italian and catholic traditions is that we don't eat any meat on Christmas Eve until after midnight, at which time we eat again. This time it was homemade plump, juicy Italian sausage, wrapped in aluminum foil, and cooked to perfection inside a blazing hot fire in the fireplace; the aroma was decadent.

While these were cooking we all sat around the fire and enjoyed roasting chestnuts on the open fire. When the Italian sausage was done, we placed them inside fresh, hot, sourdough rolls, with the juices spilling over the edges of the golden brown crust. In addition, to think that on Christmas Day, we would have an entirely new menu with the favored homemade raviolis!

It was already after midnight, and we were back home. Millie had had her bubble bath, and had her adorable, new reindeer pajamas on; we always got new holiday pajamas to wear on Christmas Eve. Before tucking Millie into bed, she had to put the cookies and milk out for Santa and a couple of carrots for his reindeers. Michael and I read her an adorable "Night before Christmas" bedtime story, and tucked her snugly into bed for the night. Once she was asleep, Santa and his elves would get right to work; those elves were

Michael and I, and our new friends across the courtyard, Nancy and Tom. They didn't have any children yet but had sure grown fond of Millie, and her of them, since we all moved in around the same time. Millie ran over to visit Nancy almost every day, and would have a great time playing with their dog.

Millie was finally asleep, and the elves were moving into action. We had our work cut out for us that night. Santa Claus and his elves were working hard to put together this outrageous swing/gym set for Millie; actually, Michael, Tom, and Nancy did all the assembling. I stood by to guard Millie's bedroom, and make sure she didn't wake up and catch Santa and his elves during the assembly. She was going to be so excited.

"It's awesome! Millie is going to have so much fun on her new swing set." We had to wake her up, and let her peak out the window to see what Santa had brought her from the North Pole!

She was sleeping like a darling little angel, but I had to gently wake her. Michael, Nancy, and Tom were hiding down the hall and enjoying every moment of this. So... with the soft whisper of my voice, and a gentle little kiss on her soft, pink, heart-shaped lips, I started to wake her up. *"Millie...wake up...Santa has already been here. You should look out your window."*

Well, it didn't take long to wake her. She sat up, gave me a big hug, and looked at me with those big, beautiful, brown eyes, long locks of golden-brown hair, and rosy cheeks. As she walked over and looked out her window, she started to scream. "He brought it, Santa really brought me my swing set! I knew he would! I just knew it!"

It was two a.m., but of course Millie wanted to go on her swing, although I managed to convince her that Santa may not be finished yet, and that she should go back to sleep until morning. It was truly heartwarming to share in the joys of Christmas with our little girl; it really was magical.

I was now into my seventh month of pregnancy, and looked pretty much like a baby elephant. Michael, Millie, and the rest of our family and friends were so excited that my pregnancy had finally made it past the critical stages. Both Millie and Michael enjoyed rubbing my tummy, and watching the movements our baby made from inside; it was truly fascinating to watch as well as feel. I often though what a blessing it was to have a baby living, breathing, and growing in my tummy; a precious miracle.

It was early one Tuesday evening, and cousin DeeDee was giving me another baby shower. As usual, all of us women were having the time of our lives. Her house was lavishly decorated for the occasion in soft, warm pastels.

The baby gifts sitting around the stork were enough to fill any nursery. And, oh my goodness, the food! There was homemade pizza, piled high with a variety of delicious meats and cheeses, enormous sourdough rounds carved out and filled with creamy mouthwatering spinach dip, delicious taco dip made with refried beans, thick-bodied guacamole, rich, sour cream, mounds of sharp cheddar cheese, spicy, diced green chilies, juicy, sliced black olives, and red roma tomatoes, with crunchy corn and flour tortilla chips for dipping. Rich, creamy clam dip with chunks of clams, and a variety of other hardy, delectable dishes.

Last but not least, the part that should always come before the main course, dessert! The cake was vanilla and chocolate marble, filled with luscious custard, and topped with snowy white, exquisite whipped cream. The decorations made it almost too adorable to eat. It really didn't look like I needed any more food; I could hardly fit into the shiny, white maple rocking chair DeeDee had decorated for me to sit on. Oh, the joys of pregnancy! My waistline was much bigger than it had been when I was carrying Millie. Actually, I had outgrown my Victoria's Secret collection and was now wearing JC Penney's men's department flannels, which were gigantic!

21

It was April 23, 1987 and Michael, Millie, and I were on our way to the hospital. Even though I hadn't had any signs of labor, my doctor wanted to induce me on my due date, so that the baby didn't get too big and cause me delivery problems, like with Millie. Once again, grandmas, aunts, cousins, and friends joined us at the hospital.

The nurse started an IV with some medicine that would induce my labor, which was followed by the doctor breaking my water. Shortly afterwards, my labor pains became very intense; I tried to remember how to do the Lamaze breathing, but it didn't seem to do any good. I couldn't concentrate on the breathing because my body was writhing out of control from the contractions.

The contractions were swift, vehement, and off the monitor in strength. Once again, I had reached delirium, and the pain was unbearable. All I kept saying was, *"Oh, God, please make the pain stop, please make it go away."*

Yeah, like that was going to happen; the only way the pain was going to stop was to deliver the baby! I realized that before I got to see my beautiful, little newborn, I was once again going to have to endure the pain of natural childbirth. I hoped they had tape ready to cover my mouth.

Several hours had passed and I thought that dying would be better than the torture I was enduring. Although I had my coaches, Michael and DeeDee, they were losing their minds trying to make me comfortable. I must have been crazy to let my doctor talk me into natural childbirth again; I should have asked for an epidural before the pain became so intense. Now, I was begging them, but it was too late; they wouldn't give me one because I was already nine centimeters dilated, and almost ready to deliver.

I felt as if a Sherman tank was trying to break through my bottom side! *"Oh, please, just let me die, I can't do this anymore!"* The labor and delivery nurses rushed me down the hall into the delivery room. *"I know they are thinking they should have had duct tape ready to keep me from screaming."* Push, push, push, gritting my teeth, trying to breathe and push. *"Are they crazy?"* I was now on the borderline of crossing over to the other side; this was a different kind of out-of-body experience, the kind where you leave the real world, and cross over into insanity!

"Oh, my God, what is that?" I had to be in control, but I wasn't, and I saw an enormous hypodermic needle coming at me. *"Are they serious? You are going to put that where?"* Well, anyone that has given birth will know exactly where that goes. Ironically, it is supposed to help you "not feel the pain" from the episiotomy, but that is after you have passed out cold from the pain the needle causes. Of course, you won't feel the episiotomy!

You will have already dropped dead from the six-inch needle!

22

It was five fifty-two p.m., and the piercing sound of screaming was gone. *"Thank God!"* All we could hear now was the joyous sound of our baby's first cry. I could hear my doctor say, "Congratulations, Sara, you have yourself another beautiful little girl!" The doctor cut the cord, and placed her onto my tummy, *"Oh, my goodness, what a wonderful feeling this is!"* Michael was standing there once again in a daze, and DeeDee was almost passed out. *"Look at her, Michael, she is so precious."*

Because she had undergone so much excess pressure coming through the birth canal, her little eyes were almost completely swollen shut. She had a few tufts of golden-brown hair, adorable puffy cheeks, and her little pink lips were puckered up and just perfect; all the things a mommy looks for were there. Ten precious little toes and fingers with glossy, delicate nails. She weighed seven pounds five ounces, and was about nineteen and a quarter inches tall. God bless her, she actually felt more like twenty pounds being delivered! She was such an adorable little butterball, and in my eyes, just perfect.

Michael, Millie, and I had decided that our new little baby's name would be Madeline and so Madeline it was. You could just see the joy in Millie's eyes when she held Madeline for the first time next to me on top of the bed. Millie gently kissed her new baby sister's soft, little cheeks. After three days, Madeline and I were able to come home from the hospital, and it was such a joy to be home with my husband and my now two precious little girls.

I let Millie help with Madeline as much as possible; she really enjoyed playing mommy, helping with Madeline's bathing, dressing, diapering, and feeding. Well, maybe not the feeding because I was breastfeeding; breastfeeding Madeline was a grin-and-bear-it situation. She had such suction; I doubted that I was going to have anything left before long!

I just loved to watch Millie holding Madeline in her arms; they both enjoyed it so much, especially Madeline, who couldn't have been more content all snuggled up in her big sister's arms, so full of love. When I thought back to how we almost lost Madeline during the pregnancy, I just couldn't imagine being without her.

23

Summer was in the air and we certainly were enjoying our two little girls. Madeline was already over two months old, and Millie would soon turn five. Michael and I were celebrating our sixth wedding anniversary, so Millie and Madeline spent the evening with Grandma and Grandpa.

Michael and I were going to our favorite restaurant, The Velvet Turtle. This restaurant was plush and "fit for the gods." A bit pricey, but we only had dinner there on very special occasions, such as this. They had a dress code so we got to dress up! Michael wore dark blue slacks, with a pinstriped blue and white long-sleeve shirt, accompanied by a deep royal-blue silk tie, while I wore a royal blue, knee length, short-sleeve silk dress, and matching royal blue ankle-strap high heels. Since it was summer, we didn't need our coats that evening.

We started our evening with a very romantic aura in a cozy little candlelit booth. As we waited for our dinner to arrive, we each enjoyed a glass of fine, Italian white wine, which only added to the already sensual mood of the evening.

We each started with a salad, which the waitress tossed in a very large salad bowl at our table; each of our salads looked like it contained an entire head of romaine lettuce, cut up into bountiful portions, smothered in rich, creamy, pungent

Roquefort dressing, and covered with chunky seasoned croutons, and just a touch of freshly ground pepper.

Could you think of a better way to enjoy these salads than with piping hot sourdough bread? As if we would have any room after that to eat our main course, a colossal Maine lobster tail with a generous portion of melted butter, already highly pleasing to the senses, accompanied by a husky Idaho baked potato piled high with butter, mounds of sour cream, and sprinkled with chives, along with fresh cut green beans, sautéed in a rich buttery garlic sauce. *"We have to save some room for dessert! The dessert here is always so divine."*

After dinner we ordered dessert; Michael had the chocolate fudge turtle brownie, with rich, hot, caramel sandwiched in between the layers, covered with crunchy chopped pecans, and topped with a generous heap of fudge, piled high with delicious fluffy whipped cream, more pecans, and a plump, juicy maraschino cherry. *"Oh, my goodness, just looking at this makes me want to reach for my antacids."* I had the chocolate mousse; rich, dark, creamy, and swirled like a tornado in a long-stemmed crystal dessert glass, smothered with fluffy whipped cream, topped with a dark chocolate-dipped maraschino cherry, stem intact, and sprinkled with crushed walnuts. After all the delectable food, I didn't think we would be able to get up from our cozy, little booth.

We hadn't had too much time for intimacy with our two precious little girls. However, that night our girls were with their grandparents, and we were spending some quality time together on our anniversary; so far, our evening had been piquant.

For us, the night was still early as we enjoyed each other's company in the privacy of our bedroom, with no lights on, save that of the moon shining through the panes of the French doors. We started our romantic interlude with a little wine, some soft, yet intoxicating mood music, and the two of us together in an impassioned exaltation of mind and feelings.

It seemed like yesterday that we were skating hand-in-hand, getting lost in each other's eyes; we never imagined that night that we would end up as husband and wife, and the proud parents of two beautiful little girls.

24

"Madeline, can you hear me? Why aren't you responding? Madeline, look it's Mommy!" My heart was beating wildly, and felt as if it was going to leave my chest. I gently picked Madeline up off my bed, trying everything possible to get her to respond. *"Oh, my God, she can't hear me!"*

Like a mother that's gone all together insane, I called our pediatrician's office crying hysterically. *"This is Mrs. Tenaci, it's about Madeline, she can't hear me, Madeline is looking at me, and can't hear me! No matter what I do, or what sounds I make, she doesn't hear it! I think there is something wrong with her hearing!"* The nurse tried to get me to calm down, and asked that I bring her into the doctor's office immediately.

Millie was already in school, and Michael was at work, so it was just Madeline and I at home; there I was crying hysterically and praying, *"Please God, don't let there be anything wrong with Madeline!"* I was cuddling her, and shaking frantically, taking deep breaths, and trying desperately to maintain my composure.

Madeline was happy as usual, kicking her little arms and legs inside her buttercup yellow sleepers. She looked like an angel with her chubby, rosy, little cheeks and warm, bright smile; she had no idea what was happening.

I bundled her up lightly, and took her to see our pediatrician. There were numerous other children in the waiting room playing with all sorts of noisy toys, but Madeline didn't seem to hear any of them. She just continued to cuddle on my lap, and not even the startling noise of the choo-choo train, or the other children screaming got her attention.

"What am I going to do?" I had all these horrible thoughts racing through my head. *"Is she going to have to go to special schools when she gets older?"* The time went by much too slowly, and as I sat there trying to be patient and wait my turn, hugging my little darling, I just couldn't hold back the tears.

Minutes later, although it seemed like hours, we were called into an exam room. Dr. Bob came in, pleasant as always, and started talking to us. I could see in his eyes that he was worried; Madeline hadn't even acknowledged that he was in the room.

I gently handed her to him, and he laid her down on the exam table to examine her ears. I was so frightened, and really didn't want to hear what he was going to tell me.

After careful examination, he said, "I don't see anything obvious." He made some noises by carefully banging and dropping things, as well as talking to her, without any response whatsoever. Now, I was really losing my mind; his look was, without doubt, one of concern. All I could think of was that my baby was deaf, and the salty tears continued to roll down my cheeks. The doctor then handed her to me, and while I was trying to prepare myself for the most earth shattering news, he said, "Hold on a second," and walked to the door.

25

As he opened, and then gently closed the door, just hard enough to make a slight noise, Madeline turned to look at him. For the first time that day, she had responded. *"Oh, thank goodness, she heard that!"* Madeline was not deaf; she really was going to be all right. Poor baby was probably trying to figure out why Mommy had this bear hug on her, and was wetting her with tears. Dr. Bob explained that even though we respond to certain sounds and noises, babies, even those with perfect hearing, don't always do that. He said, "I think she is going to be just fine." *"Thank God, what a relief!"*

It was already mid-summer and the weather was scorching. It was my brother's wedding day; he was getting married to a wonderful, young woman named Maria. Millie, Michael, and I were all in the bridal party; Madeline was comfortable being snuggled by various relatives while the ceremony was taking place. She looked so adorable with her curly, golden locks, chubby, rosy cheeks, olive-shaped, big, brown eyes, and precious smile. I had dressed her in a frilly, pink dress, trimmed with soft, white lace; it was too hot for tights, so I put on her nylon, white, frilly socks, and white patent leather shoes, and she was just precious.

This Italian Catholic wedding had all the glitz and glamor of Hollywood; our chariot, or should I say the pearly-white Rolls Royce, driven by our chauffeur, Jonathan, took Maria, her sister, Rose, Millie, and myself to the church. The rest of the bridal party arrived in limousines.

My brother looked very handsome in his coal black tuxedo with tails, white on white shirt, and black bowtie. His smile that day was one of a man in love; his smile could have lit up the sky, and as for the bride, Maria, she looked simply gorgeous in her long, flowing, pure-white silk dress, trimmed in fine lace and pearls. A little bit of pre-wedding jitters, but other than that, the look on her face was radiant and just as a woman in love, and about to be married, should look.

Ms. Millie, our little princess, looked like the "Belle of the Ball" with her hoop-style, snowy white, chiffon and lace dress trimmed with satin and pearls, that brought out her beautiful smile, big, luminous, brown eyes, and long, golden-brown hair hanging past her bottom. Millie had never been a flower girl before, and was just bubbling over with an abundance of excitement.

Michael looked handsome in his black tuxedo with tails, white on white shirt, and a deep aqua-blue bowtie and cummerbund. I wore an elegant, satin, deep aqua-blue dress, that sat off the shoulders, and had a low neckline; I felt like I had been poured into it though, considering I had just had Madeline three months earlier. Michael was pleased to see that due to the increase in my bust size from the pregnancy and breastfeeding, I was a little too well endowed for the dress… *"Okay, Michael, this is a wedding, keep your eyes in their sockets, and behave yourself!"*

The wedding was beautiful, and we had a wonderful time. Our youngest little princess, Madeline, was spoiled rotten by everyone throughout the day; she even had a chance to dance, well, with us holding her. She seemed to really enjoy being smothered with all those hugs and kisses. The bride and groom were going to Europe on their honeymoon, where they would have the time of their lives, especially when they went to Italy.

I thought I had done a bit too much dancing at the wedding, because I was exhausted, but pregnancy really takes a toll on a woman's body, along with having two little girls, one an infant, also takes a lot out of you. I knew I was going to have to take it easy.

I didn't abuse my body, no drugs, and I wasn't much of a drinker; perhaps the only thing I had done to abuse my body was go to the tanning spa, but after all those miscarriages, I needed something to make me feel better. But perhaps it made me sick? Maybe that was it; tanning every day for half an hour couldn't be good for you, my skin looked unbelievably tanned, like I had been to the French Riviera, or some other tropical island. It sure made me feel good about myself though, and I did need the morale boost.

Day by day, I continued to feel extremely lethargic, and decided it was time to see my doctor. Several blood tests revealed that I had what's called "Hashimoto's Disease."

I thought my heart had taken a sudden leave of absence from my chest. *"What in the world is that?"* I asked. The doctor said, "It's not fatal, but it does cause some unpleasant symptoms, and is a form of hypothyroidism."

So, the good news was that it wasn't fatal, but I would have to take thyroid supplements to combat the symptoms.

Madeline's first year had come and gone; it was hard to believe she was one already. She and Millie had the run of the house, and Michael and I thoroughly enjoyed our two little girls. Trips to the park, playing in our backyard on the swings, teeter tooter, bikes, the sandbox, amusement parks, the list was endless, but our real quality time was when we got to cuddle up on the couch with our two girls, and read them bedtime stories. Sometimes they didn't quite make it through the story, and we ended up carrying them to bed, which we enjoyed so much.

Putting my two adorable little ones to bed every night, and tucking them in with lots of hugs and kisses; there wasn't anything more precious in the whole world.

The three of us loved to bake cookies together, although by the time the dough was ready to be put into the pans, Millie and Madeline had eaten most of it. Well, I would have a taste here and there too, especially with Madeline always wanting Mommy to taste the dough, and shoving it in, and all around, my mouth. It was too cute for words.

26

Michael and I had celebrated our sixth wedding anniversary the previous month, Madeline was fifteen months old, and Millie would be six years old in a couple months time; life was good for all of us, with the exception of me having started to feel nauseated, tired, and very sensitive. *"Oh, I guess it will pass, it's probably the thyroid problem again. After all, I have been busy with the girls having fun with all of our summer activities."*

"Do you think? Nah, well maybe...I did miss a period, and maybe this is our little number three trying to get my attention?" It was early evening, and time to take a home pregnancy test, to see if this nausea was my thyroid acting up, or a new baby.

I had taken so many pregnancy tests in the past that I could do it with my eyes closed by then. Well, there was no question about it; the little dipstick turned blue, which meant that I was pregnant. Michael and I were thrilled, although I don't think he was as thrilled as I was, simply because my previous several pregnancies had all been so difficult.

Millie and Madeline were very excited when we told them, although Madeline was still too young to understand what was going on. After all, she was just a toddler.

The next morning I went in to see my obstetrician to take one of their pregnancy tests, just to confirm the pregnancy. My doctor put me onto progesterone hormones, just as he had with Madeline, to avoid any miscarriages or other problems. Once again, the first three months were a very critical time in the pregnancy, and although very exciting for us, this would indeed be a very stressful time in trying to make sure everything went smoothly.

As with my other pregnancies, I had many cravings; I especially liked foods that were either spicy or pungent. With Millie, I craved artichokes and almost everything, including the kitchen sink, and with Madeline, I craved all starchy foods like pastas and potatoes, which explained why I looked like a big potato.

Michael and I were going to Lake Tahoe with two very close friends of ours, Ann and Joe; we tried to get away at least for a couple of days every summer.

Millie and Madeline were excited because they got to spend the weekend with Grandma and Grandpa, which to them was like their vacation. In addition, Grandma was going to be with them, and she just adored them and spoilt them rotten. Therefore, with three grandparents, they would no doubt have a fun-filled weekend.

We drove down Highway 50, which has eight thousand foot elevation cliffs with no barriers. It made me as crazy as a loon; when I was younger, I was always able to drive it, even during the winter snowstorms, but then I felt like we were going to drive right over the edge! *"I must have a phobia."*

While driving, we actually tried to joke about it thinking it would make me feel more comfortable, but as we got closer to the peak, I started to come unglued at the seams. *"Oh, my God, oh, my God!"* Michael kept saying, "Hon, would you please calm down!"

Ann and I laughed a little, but cry and scream was what I really wanted to do. So, she got one of our goose down pillows, placed it in front of my face, and told me not to look. Yeah, easy for them to say! My nervous laughter and anxiety caused me to break out into a cold sweat. Suddenly, I heard Ann say, "Lock the doors, she's going to jump!" Well, when she said this, it really broke the ice. You could hear the explosive sound of the four of us laughing hysterically.

By the time we all pulled ourselves together, we were beyond the cliffs, and headed down the mountains into the valley. Between me losing my marbles, and Ann's sense of humor, it's a wonder how Michael was even able to drive us safely past the cliffs. Honestly, I don't know how I didn't give birth right up on the cliffs! I could see the headlines, *Woman gives birth while losing her marbles!*

Lake Tahoe was just breathtaking with the bright, summer sun shining over the glistening, crystal clear, blue lake, and the air so fresh and pleasing that we felt like we were in heaven.

We did a lot of sightseeing, rode the horse and buggy around a portion of the picturesque south shore of the lake, saw a couple of dinner and cocktail shows, and went swimming. I know, me swimming while pregnant. Now that was a sight for sore eyes.

What I really wanted to do was jet ski; I had always wanted to, and Michael just kind of went with the flow of things, and didn't care whether I did or not. However, our friends were just about ready to choke me even for thinking about jet skiing, especially considering my condition, and my history with miscarriages.

The weather was quite windy, and there had actually been a raindrop or two. Well, guess who won? Papa Joe said, "Are you crazy? There is no way I'm letting you on one of those things!" Just like craving some kind of special food, I had just really wanted to jet ski. Darn... maybe next summer.

Even though I didn't jet ski, it was one of the best weekends the four of us had ever spent together. Whenever we were together there was always tons of fun, and an everlasting flow of laughter.

27

Millie and Madeline were so happy to have Michael and I back home; Michael and I also missed them very much. I was scared to death because I had started to have cramping accompanied by spotting, which was not a good sign for me. There we went again, back to my doctor's office. And once again, he told me he would increase the progesterone hormone, but if that didn't work, we would have no other options, except just to let nature take its course. I didn't think I could take another heartbreak.

A couple of weeks had passed, and it was time for my amniocentesis. *"Oh, my goodness, I don't think I want them sticking that long needle into my tummy, and besides it hurting, what if they hit my baby?"*

Can you believe the stuff us women have to endure? I thought I was going to shake right out of my shoes. Michael came into the exam room with me, and after they prepared my tummy for the dreaded procedure, he held my hand, and tried to comfort me as much as possible.

After cleaning my watermelon-sized tummy, the doctor used an ultrasound while inserting the needle. It actually looked more like a barbeque skewer than a needle. *"Lord, have mercy, I'm not a chicken! Well, maybe I am a chicken but not for barbeque!"* I was very apprehensive about this procedure, and had to try to be tolerant of the discomfort. The doctor asked if we would like to know what the sex of the baby was; I guessed they could tell from the ultrasound, not the amnio, because that takes three weeks to confirm all findings.

"No, we don't want to know what the sex of our baby is and besides, I have a funny feeling that it is another girl anyway."

Three weeks later I got a phone called from the clinic where I had had the amnio. I was delighted with the good news; my test revealed a healthy baby with no anomalous findings. *"Now if I can just get through my pregnancy without having a miscarriage... that would be a blessing."*

Again, the doctor asked if I would like to know the sex of our baby. I said, *"I already know what it is."* He said, "You do?" "I said, *"Yes, I have always felt like I was going to have all little girls."* He chuckled and said, "Well, you are right, you have yourself another little girl!"

I was overwhelmed with this news, not only was my baby healthy, but it was another precious little girl! *"Wow, another sister, Millie and Madeline are going to be so excited."* Michael, well, he was never a macho man about wanting to have a son; he was perfectly content with all little girls, and would be relieved to hear that our baby was another healthy, little girl.

When Michael got home from work, I told him the good news, and his face lit up with joy. Michael, as well as everyone else, thought I was carrying a little boy because of my "basketball-out-front" look.

Now, even after telling everyone that we knew the baby was a little girl, they still disagreed and relentlessly insisted it was a boy. An amnio is ninety-nine percent accurate, so I would let them think what they wanted to. This pregnancy would be the last one for us; Michael and I had decided a long time ago that we wanted three children, regardless of whether they were boys or girls.

My tummy had already grown to a significant size, and I was only in my fifth month, and was still taking the hormones to sustain my pregnancy.

Meanwhile, Millie was testing the waters at school. She didn't really care for her teacher; they seemed to have a bit of a personality clash. Stubborn? No, not my Millie! Although a wonderfully precious and loving child, she was actually quite headstrong.

Everyday when I picked her up from school, she would be crying; she was extremely unhappy with her teacher, and St. Lucy's. She had always been stubborn and I couldn't imagine where she got that from; Madeline was quite the opposite in personality, so far anyway, and was very passive in nature.

Madeline and I would just go through our regular routine, waiting for Millie to get out of school and having fun, which was very important. Madeline and I really missed Millie when she was at school.

Madeline was always looking at my tummy, and trying to figure out why it was growing so enormous; she loved to sit on my lap, and rub my tummy. She would even put her little ear delicately onto my tummy to see if she could hear anything, and when she did hear the unimaginable sounds coming from within, her beautiful, bright, brown eyes lit up, and her expression was priceless.

She would whisper, so as not to wake the baby, which was so cute. She and Millie thought they had a new toy in my tummy.

One day Madeline was with me in the kitchen, and then she disappeared. When I realized she was gone I wasn't too worried, as the house had been childproofed. I figured she was probably in her bedroom playing with her toys, but I went to check anyway. She wasn't in her room, or in Millie's room; she must be in my room. So I went into my bedroom, and saw her sitting in my closet, with a dubious look on her face. *"Hey, little stinker, there you are. What are you up to?"*

I immediately noticed something unusual inside of her mouth. I wasn't sure what it could possibly be since she was sitting amongst all of my shoes.

So, I asked, *"Madeline, can you please give Mommy what you have in your mouth?"* Without any hesitation, she pulled this little white packet with crossbones on it out of her delicate, little mouth.

"Oh, my God, Madeline! You had poison in your mouth!" She had taken one of those preservative packets out of one of my shoeboxes, and was trying to eat it. I immediately picked her up, placed her in my arms with her petite little legs wrapped around my colossal belly, and started running down the hall screaming. *"Oh, my God, please God, don't let her die!"*

As I ran around the house like a maniac, Madeline just held on for dear life. After all, she was just a toddler, and had no idea why her Mommy was screaming, and probably thought it was just another game!

I went into the kitchen, and yanked open the cabinet to look at my emergency numbers list. *"I will call Poison Control, they will know what to do."* I was crying hysterically, and trying to tell whomever I was talking to that my baby just ate a poison packet! *"What should I do? Please tell me what to do, and that she is going to be okay?"*

28

Madeline was going to be just fine, thank God. Poison Control said just to give her a little bit of milk, and to follow up with our pediatrician, which I did. The shock of that incident was enough to make me go into premature labor. Soon after that, I started cramping and spotting again, and every time I stood up, it felt like my bottom was going to drop out. I was only five months pregnant, and couldn't be going into labor yet, it was much too soon; if I went into labor then my baby would most certainly have died.

I went in to see my doctor, and he advised me that it was, in fact, too soon to deliver. However, should I start having more severe cramping, or contractions, I must head over to the hospital immediately.

A few days later, the little pains had turned into contractions, at regular five-minute intervals. Now I really felt like my bottom was falling out. *"This can't be happening again!"*

A friend of ours happened to be over and said, "That's it, we are going to the hospital," and in less than half an hour, she and the nurses were wheeling me expeditiously into labor and delivery, with Millie and Madeline at my side. Michael was still at work, and had no idea that anything was happening.

My heart was now racing out of control; they immediately put me into a bed, and hooked up all the monitors. My girls were really alarmed by all of this. I tried to comfort them, by telling them that Mommy and baby were going to be just fine, while at the same time feeling like I was losing my marbles.

My nurse wanted me to try to calm down. *"Yeah, right, you calm down when you are only five months pregnant, and have a history of six miscarriages."* I didn't tell her that, but I sure wanted to. My contractions were very consistent at five minutes apart; the nurse alerted both my obstetrician and our pediatrician.

The nurse performed an ultrasound, although she wouldn't elaborate. But, the fetal monitor indicated the baby was doing just fine, and not under any stress. After spending a couple of hours in the hospital hooked up to all kinds of monitors and such, they let me return home with strict orders. I figured it was in God's hands now, and would just continue to pray.

The holidays were getting closer, and it was an extremely busy time of year for all of us. I was no doubt pleasingly plump and exceedingly uncomfortable.

One morning, Millie, Madeline, and I had a few errands to run. So I got the girls ready, set the alarm on the house, and headed out the door. Suddenly, as I walked out of the door, I fell off the porch, landing face down on my very pregnant tummy.

As I lay on the ground, I slowly felt myself coming to my senses; I was crying, and I could hear my two little girls screaming, "Mommy, Mommy, are you okay?" I hurt pretty badly, and my two little darlings were trying to pick their larger-than-life Mommy off the ground, which wasn't working too well. I was totally dazed from the fall, and think perhaps I had just blacked out; my hands and knees were scraped up pretty bad, but my main concern was for the baby.

Well, Millie got on the phone and called Grandma. Fortunately, she only lived down the street, and made it to our house in a heartbeat. She was scared to death seeing me in that condition. We immediately all got into the car, and went to the doctor, who examined me, and used the ultrasound to check the baby's heartbeat; everything appeared to be fine. It seemed there was always something to scare the life, or the baby, right out of me.

I was seven months pregnant, and counting. Life seemed to be going smoothly, and my pregnancy was still hanging in there, literally. We had a flotation mattress, and since I was so large, I often needed help from Michael to get into bed, and to turn over; kind of like a beached baby whale.

At night, we would lie in bed, fascinated by our baby moving from one side of my tummy to the other, and sometimes I would have several contractions. Michael liked to rub my tummy, and the baby seemed to like it as well. I know I enjoyed it, as it was relaxing for me just lying snuggled up next to him. Every evening around eleven o'clock she would put on a little show for us, moving all over the place, almost as if she knew we were lying in bed, and she had our undivided attention.

Michael's mom had been diagnosed with cancer some time earlier, but he had had a nice conversation with her that particular week, and she was feeling good, doing one of her favorite things, which was decorating for the holidays. Several days later, at two a.m., the phone rang. You always know when you are sound asleep and you hear the phone ring, that no one is calling you to go out for a cup of coffee, and that it has to be heavyhearted news. I rolled my plump, not-so-little body over, and grabbed the phone.

A very melancholy voice said, "Sara." I said, *"Who is this?"* Suddenly the little voice broke into tears, and said, "It's me, Jessica, Mom just died." I said, *"What? We didn't even know that she was in the hospital! Why didn't you guys call your brother and tell him?"* Her reply was, "I don't know."

Michael woke up, and asked what was going on. I said, *"Michael, it's Jessica, your Mom just died!"* Michael, as one would expect, started to cry. I tried to comfort him, but there never seems to be the right words at a time like that.

I couldn't believe that his five siblings hadn't the fortitude to call him to say their Mom was in the hospital, dying! What was the matter with them? Actually, it shouldn't have surprised me, though, considering how they had always treated him as if he were the black sheep of the family. All of her children had been by her side when she passed away, except for her eldest son; there was something wrong with that picture. That was a long, sorrowful evening for us, especially for Michael; now his mother was gone, and he had never even known his father.

The following day I went along with Michael to the hospital morgue for moral support. The nurse told us that they would bring Michael's mom into a side room of the morgue for him to see her, and not to be alarmed because they hadn't done anything to her yet. Michael was a nervous wreck, and my legs were like Jell-O.

Saying they had not done anything to her was quite an understatement; Michael and I walked into the undersized, vacuous, white-walled room. It was cold, really cold, just like death. I felt like all my blood had been drained from my body. They rolled her into the room on a rusty stainless steel gurney, and as soon as Michael and I saw her, we both started to cry.

He stood there as if in a daze, while the tears flowed down his cheeks. They hadn't even taken time to cover her frail little body; she had what appeared to be a white sheet on part of her so, out of respect, I gently grabbed the sheet and covered all of her with it, except for her face.

I couldn't believe what I was seeing! Here was my mother-in-law, weighing maybe sixty-five to seventy pounds of basically skin and bones. Her big, beautiful, blue-green eyes were still open, as was her mouth; the hospital staff didn't even have sense enough to close her eyes. Her little body was frozen in a somewhat sitting position, and had obviously buckled, gasping for that last breath of air. God rest her soul, and forgive me for saying this, but she looked like something from a horror movie... it just made me sick; the cancer had obviously destroyed her.

The nurse was holding me up, I guess in my very pregnant condition she hadn't wanted me to pass out. Michael shouldn't have had to see his Mom that way; it was loathsome that the hospital should be allowed to carry on like that with so little preparation.

In the next couple of days, Michael met with his family, we went to a memorial service, and then he attended the private burial with his siblings. My mother-in-law had wanted to be cremated, and wished for her ashes to be spread out over the ocean.

All six of her children took her cremated remains, and drove up the coast. They stopped when they reached a cliff with enormous waves rushing in from the sea, thundering against its face. This would be where they would set her soul free. And so it was; her ashes were tossed, and spilled out gently into the swift ocean breeze, into the thundering sound of the waves crashing against the mammoth rocks. The six of them watched and prayed, as their Mom's remains seemed to disappear into the essence of the salt air.

29

As we tried to get back to normal, I kept wondering what normal really was. I was in my eighth month of pregnancy and there was no holding back; my mucous plug, contractions, and everything that goes with having a baby had begun. We had to call Michael at work, he had just left about half an hour earlier, and I hadn't had any signs at that time. Michael was going to have to meet us at the hospital, because I was in labor, and this little girl was not waiting.

There we were, Mom, aunts, and Grandma, a bunch of little Italian nerves running around my kitchen trying to get me ready to leave. Once we arrived at the hospital, the nurses rushed me into labor and delivery. This was it, and my doctor had arrived promptly.

Knowing that this was my ninth pregnancy, and the fact that this baby had been trying to be born for several months already, they weren't taking any chances. The labor was starting to get intense, although my waters hadn't broken yet.

So, my doctor wanted to break my water. There I was in the middle of very intense contractions, doing that bizarre breathing I had been taught, screaming at the same time, and he wanted to do what? *"Do you have to do that right now?"* Well, it wasn't as if he was giving me a choice.

The IV was in place, and the doctor gave me more medicine to induce the labor even further. The contractions, and back labor became unbearable and, only being dilated to seven, I didn't think I could take much more.

Once again, Michael and DeeDee were my coaches. The doctor was standing by, and administered a partial Para cervical block to give me a little relief. It wasn't working too well, and I really had the urge to push.

The nurses would not allow me to push yet, as I was not dilated enough, and would tear my cervix. So, they give me the other half of the Para cervical block, which lasted probably less than half an hour. I felt like the earth wanted to move out through my bottom! I was screaming... in control of this situation? I don't think so!

When my cervix didn't seem to be making any more progress, the doctor thought he would leave for a while. Big mistake... I was dilated to ten, and the doctor was on his way back to the hospital in his car, and I was on my way down the hall, and it looked like the nurse would deliver my baby without the doctor. The nurses quickly put me into the delivery bed, placing all my anatomy in its proper place, and I was ready to give birth.

The situation was very intense. I couldn't wait, and felt a strong urge to push! Our pediatrician arrived, the baby was coming, and I heard the nurse say, "She's crowning!" They saw my baby's head, and I could feel the powers that be. I felt delirious, my obstetrician was finally there, and I might add, having gotten a speeding ticket on his way in. My bottom started to tear before he had a chance to start the episiotomy; he went ahead with it anyway, and with a few more pushes, I was able to push her little, well, not so little, body out into the world.

30

At six minutes past three, on January 25, 1989, once again that beautiful sound that you wait nine, well in this case eight months to hear, was finally letting the world know that she had arrived. Since my doctor had already delivered our first two little girls, he said, "You have yourself another beautiful little girl!" And, our pediatrician said, "She has a tiny little spot on her head, but don't worry."

She was precious; Michael and I were so excited. I said, *"Michael, she is here, finally safe and sound. She's perfect."* Because she was a month early, once the nurses had cleaned her, the doctors made sure all her organs were working properly before handing her to me. *"Oh, my gosh, Michael, look at her!"* Michael had that "I'm a proud Daddy" look on his face once again.

My goodness, she was chubby for being a month early, weighing in at seven pounds and seven ounces. She was just adorable with her big, beautiful, hazel eyes, and a face round and smooth like an apple, precious little lips, and a tiny little button nose.

She had golden-brown hair, but not very much of it, and a dark brown birthmark on top of her head. Her little fingers and toes were perfect. Oh, how I had worried about her during this pregnancy!

To finally hold her in my arms was truly a miracle, and to think that so many times we almost lost her. As I held her close to my heart, all wrapped up snugly in her soft, pink, baby blanket, my eyes began to well up.

Michael was gently trying to hug both of us at the same time as the two of us welcomed our new little one into the family. Madison Tenaci, our third adorable, precious little girl. Millie and Madeline were going to be so excited when they got to see their new little sister.

Once we were sure that everything was okay, Michael carried her into the nursery, where the rest of our family and friends could partake in another memorable moment. Everyone was filled with excitement, taking advantage of being able to hold her, and give gentle hugs to our new, little arrival.

It was a very unnatural feeling to be taken away from your baby, and that was exactly what had happened. I was being rolled into surgery, having to leave my precious, new little baby, and two other precious little girls, as well as Michael, behind.

31

Having your tubes tied doesn't cause postpartum blues, does it? Madison was only two days old, and I had a really serious case of the blues. I was lighthearted and heavyhearted at the same time. By the second day, I was so depressed that my doctor kept me in the hospital for an additional day.

Having a baby was one of the happiest moments of my life, so why was I so upset? My doctor tried to talk to me, and couldn't figure out how I could be so unhappy after just giving birth to another beautiful, healthy baby. He didn't understand much of what I was saying because I was crying hysterically.

I was trying desperately, between the tears, to tell him what was wrong with me. As the tears started to roll down my cheeks, I told him that I had worked so hard to have all my babies; they were truly a gift, and now what had I done? God had blessed me with three beautiful, healthy, little girls, and he would be so disappointed in me now.

My doctor stared at me dumbfounded, not really sure what to say, but he was finally starting to see the picture in living color. Being a religious man, he asked me, "Why in the world would you be thinking such a thing?" I said, *"Because, because I had my tubes tied!"* And by then, I had totally lost it... it almost seemed like a death, instead of a birth. As my emotions soared out of control, he tried to comfort me, and told me that I would feel better about my decision soon.

A few days had passed, and all five of us were trying to settle in, once again. Millie and Madeline were just thrilled with baby Madison; they loved helping with the diapers, and such, and especially enjoyed watching her have her little baths... they were fascinated, and snuggled up as close as possible when I breastfed her.

Holding the baby, with Millie and Madeline on either side was completely heartwarming. Grandma came over everyday to fill up on hugs and kisses from her three granddaughters, and to help out as much as possible.

There was still something wrong though. I was still very downhearted, and almost as if in another world. What was wrong with me? My life was a dream come true. I had three precious little girls, what more could anyone ever want?

My family was completely puzzled by my unstable emotions, and were really starting to worry. Dr. Bob, our pediatrician, knew of my depression, and had been checking in on me daily. He knew my state of mind was not so strong, but that day when he called, I could sense from the tone of his voice that he wasn't just calling to check on my mental state.

He proceeded to tell me that Madison's blood tests had revealed an abnormality, and that we would have to take her for more lab work, which would be sent to Stanford.

Cry? You'd imagine I cried, wouldn't you? Everyone had become so familiar with my constant sobbing that it didn't even faze them anymore. What was wrong with my baby? Besides being slightly jaundiced, she looked fine, and appeared to be thriving.

The next day I brought Madison to the hospital for lab work; Grandma came along for moral support, and to help me with Millie and Madeline. It was heart wrenching watching my baby have lab work, and it would be a couple of weeks yet before we got the test results back.

Meanwhile we would just continue to pray. However, within days, Madison was deteriorating right before my eyes; her coloring was shocking, and she had lost a great deal of weight.

Dear God, what was wrong with her? She looked like a cancer patient, this couldn't be happening! God was punishing me. I just knew I was being punished. I prayed, *"I know that I shouldn't have had my tubes tied, and I'm so sorry... Please don't take Madison from us. She's dying, isn't she?"*

My state of mind was so delicate that this would definitely have sent me over the edge. Poor Millie and Madeline thought Mommy had taken a leave of her senses. And Michael, well he didn't know what to think.

Finally, the two dreadful weeks of waiting had passed, and we got a call from our pediatrician with the test results. It felt as though my heart hadn't just skipped a beat, but had jumped right out of my chest. *"What do you mean? What is wrong with her? Madison is going to die, isn't she?"*

32

Dr. Bob said, "You need to stop breastfeeding Madison immediately. She has what's called 'Duarte Galactosemia,' which basically means that she is missing an enzyme in her liver, and thus cannot and won't ever be able to breakdown breast milk or any other dairy products; your breast milk is poisoning her, and continuing would be fatal. If she has a minor form of this disease, she can live a normal, highly productive life. However, if she has a major form of it, she won't live past two or three years old.

It is essential that we get more blood work from her, Michael, and you, to determine whether she has a minor or major form of this disease. The odds of a baby having this disease are one in every forty thousand, and the only way the amnio would have shown this was if we had already known it was in your family, which we didn't."

I just couldn't take this anymore! It must be true, I was being punished! Why my baby, though? Why punish my baby? Tears were in abundant supply, and seemed like they were going to be flowing forever. Everyone tried to comfort and reassure me that I was not being punished; my obstetrician was preparing to send me to a psychiatrist if my depression and mental state didn't start improving soon.

Dr. Bob still called me every day. He said, "Cry all you want to, I wish I could bottle your tears, they are the best medicine." He thought since I had an overabundance of milk, perhaps I would feel better about myself if I donated my milk to the "Mother's Milk Bank" for premature babies, which was exactly what I did. I registered with them, and donated my milk to help save the lives of hundreds of premature babies.

It had been several weeks since I stopped breastfeeding Madison, and switched her over to soy formula, and we would soon be hearing the results of the special blood tests to determine the severity of Madison's disease. She seemed to be thriving, and had gained weight since stopping my breast milk. Every day I prayed that we would get good news. She was so precious, and such a joy, and we all loved her so much.

I had decided to call and see if the results were in yet; I couldn't stand having to wait any longer! While awaiting the results, Dr. Bob had already been in contact with several of the major UC Hospitals and Medical Centers, as far as the East Coast, with regard to Madison's metabolic disease 'Duarte Galactosemia.'

Finally, I got up enough nerve to call Stanford, and our results were in fact ready. However, I was not so sure that I was ready to hear them.

The news was quite disturbing, and I paced back and forth in my kitchen. The doctor came to the phone and said, "You do understand that galactose accumulates in the blood, due to the deficiency of an enzyme in Madison's liver, the catalyst for its conversion to glucose?" I said, *"Yes, I already know that, now can you please tell me the results of the blood tests?"*

He said, "It looks like Michael carried the Galactosemia gene, and you, Sara, carried the Duarte gene, thus passing it on to Madison. She will have to be closely monitored, and we won't know for a while whether or not her restricted diet is going to work. This can be a life-threatening disease, and if the diet doesn't work, children with it can die by the age of two, or have brain damage and/or severe cataracts, which cause blindness."

It broke my heart to think that my little angel might die; I was not going to let anything happen to her. She was a beautiful, wonderful child, who had brought us so much joy, and I wouldn't let her be taken away from us. With all of our family and friends praying, we had to believe that she would recover, and have a normal childhood. Everyday my good friend Nancy, from across our courtyard, came over and visited to try to help in any way she could. Nancy and Tom had just had their first child, a little boy named Andrew, and he was just adorable.

It seemed like so much time had passed, yet Madison was still only a couple of months old. Millie and Madeline were wonderful through everything. Michael was wonderful too, but being a man, I don't think he understood what a woman goes through at a time like that.

Madison was becoming so spoilt; she seemed to have adjusted to the soy diet, and her visits to the doctor showed a significant improvement in her condition. I guess all our prayers that I didn't think would be answered, had been. Things were starting to get back to normal again, and my depression seemed to be under control.

My three daughters and I always enjoyed each other's company, whether it be reading stories, playing games, going to the park, or just cuddling; anything and everything that brought us pleasure. Michael worked a lot so we didn't see him all that often.

The sweet, gentle fragrance of star jasmines in the air was a signal that spring had arrived. Madison was being baptized by my godparents, Auntie Ella and Uncle Charlie, who meant the world to me. I thought it would be nice if Madison and I had the same godparents, and they couldn't have been more proud.

The real estate market was hot, and Michael and I had sold our house; we were on the list for a larger home, in a development not too far from where we were currently living. It was double the size of our old home, in a charming little community with unlimited amenities including a pool, cabana, and private park, which our three little ones would thoroughly enjoy.

Meanwhile, we would be renting another home until the new one was built. I had been doing some research on investing a little money in a home-based business for myself. I wanted to spend as much quality time as possible with my little girls, and be able to enjoy watching them grow up. I had found the perfect business opportunity, and purchased a dealership. I would be making "personalized children's books," which I could do on my home computer, and sell via mail order, and at festivals. This was perfect, and my girls would, no doubt, become budding, young entrepreneurs.

The summer had come and gone, and Millie was back at school; she had just turned seven, and her favorite musical interest was "New Kid's on the Block." Madeline didn't have a favorite musical interest yet, she was more interested in all the colorful little jungle animals, and baby dolls in her bedroom, and Madison liked to cuddle her fuzzy, little bears and toys, and be wherever her sisters were.

I so enjoyed watching her beautiful, big brown eyes, and face light up when Millie and Madeline were in a room with her; I was sure she was making mental notes of all this stuff.

It was already October 17, 1989. How the time did fly, it was almost Halloween, and my little goblins would soon be getting dressed up.

We had just finished dinner, and were talking about what costumes we were going to wear that year; Halloween is so much fun, especially when you have children to dress up.

"Michael, what is that noise? It sounds like a train; there are no trains in our neighborhood! Oh, my God, Michael, it's an earthquake, grab the girls!"

At four minutes past five, an earthquake measuring 7.5 on the Richter scale struck. None of us had ever endured anything so frightening in our lives! It felt as if the earth was going to swallow all of us up.

For Michael and I, the most important thing was to make sure that our girls, as well as our puppies, were unharmed. The girls were just horrified; they didn't really understand earthquakes, but what they did know is that they didn't ever want to experience another one.

The Halloween ghosts and goblins were a real treat that year, especially after living through that. Moreover, living through it is the key here; thank God none of us were physically harmed, although it definitely rattled my nerves a little too much.

Between the earthquake, keeping busy with my girls, and my personalized children's books business, I was drained. I didn't know what was wrong with me, but I thought that perhaps I should slow down a bit.

Good ole' turkeys were gobbling just around the corner. For me, Thanksgiving was the best eating day of the year, and it would be extra special for us that year as it was Madison's first Thanksgiving. We would give her a nice, juicy drumstick; she wouldn't be able to eat it, but it sure made a cute picture watching her try, just as Millie and Madeline had tried when they were babies.

That year, Thanksgiving was at Grandma and Grandpa's house, with my brother and his family, including their two little girls, so the house would be full of adorable little girls, and of course, a feast fit for royalty.

My Mom, Maria, and I did all the cooking; our colossal twenty-five pound turkey smelt sensational, it's delectable golden-brown skin cooked to perfection, with mouthwatering juices dripping in abundance onto the platter.

There were mounds of delicious Idaho potatoes, mashed with pure butter, cream, and a pinch of salt, looking like fluffy clouds, with the heat still rising up from within, a delicious, velvety, brown gravy made from the turkey juices, and other family secrets, hundreds of sweet tender peas, rich buttered carrots, stuffing made the Italian way with an aroma that just draws you in with a hint of pleasure, candied yams made with lots of golden brown sugar, pure vanilla, butter, raisins, and marshmallows, baked to a golden brown crust, and cranberry sauce so tart it made your lips pucker.

And as if this was not enough food, there were dozens of raviolis, stuffed like fluffy pillows, smothered in a thick, deep-red Italian sauce, satiated with creamy cheese fillings, as well as pungent meatballs to die for. Top all of this off with salads, breads, and desserts, and you would think that we did nothing but eat. Everything was so delectable; we had much to be thankful for, and our family was truly blessed.

33

Christmas had arrived, and it would be Madison's first. Millie and Madeline were so exhilarated and couldn't wait to see what Santa had brought them; it was all new to Madison, and when she saw our beautiful tree all lit up with lots of toys and presents under it, her big, brown eyes lit up like the moon in the midnight sky. The excitement among the three of them was just adorable.

Madison was walking now, and found it very amusing being able to toddle over to our tree, and pick up and tear open presents without any help. Our living room actually looked like Santa's Workshop with all the dolls, toys, and even a train with its own tracks that Santa had brought.

Santa had forgotten a dollhouse on the roof, shh... it must have fallen out of his bag when he was coming down the chimney. Daddy (a.k.a. Santa) would have to go onto the roof to get it down.

It was so heartwarming to see the expressions on our daughters' faces when they believed that Santa had actually dropped a toy on the roof. In addition, I might add, he left one of his boots in the fireplace. Oh, my... it must have slipped off... having children to share the holidays with was so magical, and brought us so much joy.

It was Madison's first birthday, and we were celebrating it with a fun-filled party at the park, which included a barbeque, games, and even an adorable "clown," which was actually Janet, Nancy's sister.

She was too cute in her purple, white, and green-striped clown apparel, and the kids just loved her. Madison was having a good time, but was a bit cranky; perhaps it was the cold weather, and the fact that I had her dressed up as if she were going to play in the snow. She looked like a baby Eskimo all zipped up. The only part of her not covered was her precious, rosy cheeks and big brown eyes.

I hadn't ever remembered her being that cranky; maybe she was coming down with something, she really hadn't had too much of an appetite over the previous few days or so. Then again, babies do change their eating habits, don't they? I would weigh her just to make sure she hadn't lost any weight; she was twenty-pounds, and last time had been twenty-one pounds. *"Oh, it's probably nothing,"* I thought. *"Her coloring and everything else seems fine."*

A week had passed, and it was evident that Madison was not feeling well; she had just about ceased eating altogether, and her once round, apple-shaped face seemed to have thinned out a fearful amount. A visit to the doctor confirmed she had lost four pounds, and was now only seventeen pounds at the age of one.

"Oh, my God, she is sick again!" I was totally stressed out, and the only thing I could think of was that her disease was active, and that she was going to die. The doctor did some lab work, and then all we could do was wait, and try to get her to eat and drink.

When I held and cuddled her, it felt as though I was holding a feather; she didn't even want to walk anymore, and had resorted to crawling again.

"Dear Lord, haven't we been through enough? Madison doesn't deserve to be sick and die." All I could do was keep the faith, and continue to pray for her. Over the past year, she had touched the hearts of so many. I just couldn't imagine life without her.

Madison's lab work came back and, thank goodness, everything seemed to be normal. Our doctor was puzzled as to why she had suddenly stopped thriving, but was hopeful that whatever it was would reverse itself.

Once past the hurdle of Madison's unexplained weight loss, one evening Madeline was trying to get up into a bar stool for dinner, and didn't quite make it.

Consequently, she fell back onto the unforgiving floor, and broke her arm, a compound fracture, and dislocated her elbow. This was no easy fix; our poor little darling had to have surgery, and then was placed in a cast that looked like it belonged on a doll.

Well, it did go on a doll, our little doll. I hoped that I didn't ever have to see any of our children get hurt again; it was horrifying to see this poor baby's arm, and the pain she had to go through. We always seemed to have something happening in our house. Nevertheless, I guess when you have children; you should always expect the unexpected.

With the exception of a few miscellaneous items, family life seemed to be coming along just fine. Madison had started eating like a little piggy again, and Madeline's arm had healed up good as new. Millie was quite the mini-adult, or parent figure with her two younger sisters.

Michael and I loved to sit back and watch her; it was like she was playing house, but she did a good job of it, and almost too good for such a youngster. All three of them brought us so much pleasure.

All of the stressful situations, including Madison's disease, Madeline breaking her arm, running my own home-based business etc, had taken their toll on me, and I was completely exhausted. Could stress make you feel this awful?

Michael had gone off to work but not for long; I had started trembling from head to toe. What was wrong with me now? Was I having a seizure? My entire body felt like melting Jell-O, so I thought perhaps I would just sit down, and hoped this would calm my nerves.

By this time, I was crying because I wasn't sure what was wrong, and I was so scared. I called Michael at work, and told him he needed to get home right away because there was something wrong with me.

He got home expeditiously, but by then, my body seemed to be losing control, and I was losing my mind. Michael's eyes were as big as saucers, and I could see that he was scared to death that something was happening to his wife, and it was pretty much out of his control. We called Grandma to take the girls, and Michael rushed me to the hospital.

Once in the E.R., the doctors ran some tests, but were worried and confused about my condition. Even though conscious, I was shaking as if I was having some sort of uncontrollable seizure activity. I was given an injection from a large hypodermic syringe, filled with something resembling milk, and within a few moments, my jerking body had almost calmed down to normal.

Still without a diagnosis, they told me to contact my doctor, follow up with the lab results, and sent me home.

I was fine for a day or so, and Michael had returned to work, but without any warning whatsoever, on Saturday afternoon my body once again started to tremble, only this time it was accompanied by a horrendous pain in my chest, which felt as if it were being crushed.

Once again, Michael had to rush home from work. I was screaming, and pacing briskly back and forth in the house, shaking, and totally out of my mind with the pain. I cried, *"Michael, there is something wrong with me, what is wrong with me? My chest is being crushed! Please take me to the hospital, this is not normal!"*

Once again, Grandma came to get the girls, and without any hesitation, Michael grabbed me, gently helped me into our mini-van, and we hurried to the emergency room for the second time that week.

When we arrived at the Emergency Room, the doctors were extremely flustered by my body's erratic behavior. The only thing different this time was the crushing pain in my chest, which I just couldn't tolerate.

The doctors didn't even do a cardiogram; however, more labs and more milky meds were injected into my body in an attempt to give me some relief from the symptoms.

Once again, the milky injections seemed to make the symptoms subside, but they still had no idea what was causing them, and once again sent me home with the same instructions.

I wanted to know what they were injecting into me, and why they were using it if they didn't know what they were treating? And since it was working, what did they think was wrong with me?

I saw "MS" with a question mark on the admittance sheet, with some chicken scratch, but no one would comment as to why.

The lab work revealed some abnormalities, but nothing conclusive. This was followed up with a CAT scan, to which I had an allergic reaction. Apparently, I was allergic to the iodine contrast, which caused huge red welts all over my body, and I was given meds to counteract this reaction.

Within a couple of days, we got the results of the scan, and it wasn't exactly good news. The scan revealed a mediastinal mass, and the doctors wanted to do another scan just to confirm the findings, but this time without contrast to avoid the allergic reaction. That scan did unfortunately confirm the mass.

My first thought was, *"Cancer, I must have cancer."* It was the spring of 1990, and all hell was about to break loose; my doctor had arranged for me to see a surgeon, as well as an oncologist. It was all becoming much too difficult for me to handle. I couldn't be sick; I had three little girls to raise!

Michael drove me to the oncologist first, although he preferred to sit in the car while I went in. I wasn't sure why, but okay. The whole thing had to be a bad dream, and I wished that someone would please wake me up!

I didn't care too much for the office, which was more like a morgue, and very cold, like death. The bedside manner of the doctor was like frostbite.

My heart was beating out of control, and my entire body felt like Jell-O that had just been splashed with water, and was going down the drain. I was listening to him speaking to me, but felt as if I had been anesthetized, and couldn't move or speak. I couldn't even cry...

Did I hear him say, "I think there is a strong possibility that you have lymphoma"? No, he couldn't have said that! That wasn't possible. However, that was in fact exactly what he was telling me, and that the surgeon would have to do a biopsy.

I left his office feeling like a zombie, as if in a tenebrous fog, and walked out to my car where Michael had been waiting impatiently for me. Michael never really had too much to say; you could always count on the same exact words from him every time something went wrong which were, "That's not good."

I wasn't sure why, but that day it really annoyed me, especially since I was crying, having that dreadful crushing pain in my chest, and didn't know whether I was going to live or die.

34

The waiting room in the surgeon's office was quite cheerful compared to the oncologist's office, which felt like death. After my exam, the surgeon said, "I don't want to alarm you, but you do realize that this mass is probably lymphoma, and that lymphoma is cancer?"

I nodded, and as the tears started to gush down my cheeks, I said, *"Am I going to be able to see my kids grow up?"* The answer wasn't exactly what I had hoped for though, he just put his hand on my shoulder and said, "I don't know, we will just have to wait and see what the biopsy shows."

Once again, Michael had waited for me in the car, and once again when I told him what the doctor and I had discussed, he said, "That's not good." I was crying my eyes out, thinking that this was just not fair, and that my little girls were going to grow up without a Mommy, and that was his response!

Most of my family was at our house taking care of our three little girls, and waiting for the news. When we walked into the house the mood was somber; the expressions on their faces made it apparent they could see the sadness in my eyes, and that the news was definitely tear jerking.

It was an extremely emotional time for all of us; everyone was crying and screaming, including me, and my Mom was down the hall throwing up. My babies had no idea what lymphoma was, and I was not about to tell them. Once we had all regained our composure, we did what most Italians do in a crisis; we eat! The aroma of fresh Italian sausage on sourdough rolls didn't take away the emotional pain, it only served as a little bit of a diversion.

A couple of days later, I had my biopsy, and my doctors had me out of the hospital within two days. I had quite an entourage of family and friends supporting me. Now we would have to wait three days for the biopsy results. The time just seemed to be dragging along at a snail's pace. All I kept saying was, *"Please God, don't let it be lymphoma!"* I want to be here with, and for, my little girls.

35

The news was good; the mass was not lymphoma, thank God! However, the biopsy was not conclusive, which meant more diagnostic testing for me. As long as I knew that I was going to be here to love and raise my little girls, I could handle anything.

Life seemed to be coming along beautifully, and our little girls were growing up right before our eyes. I felt blessed to have them, and cherished every precious moment with them. Soon we would be moving into our new home, the one that was being built, with the pool, spa, and private park.

The girls were so excited. Michael and I only had until June of 1991 to repurchase, to avoid capital gains tax from the sale of our previous home. Our finances were solid with one hundred thousand dollars in the bank, plus investments in the stock market. We had done pretty well for ourselves.

It had been a while since Michael's mom had passed on, and occasionally we would discuss his father. He often wondered where he was, and what had happened to him. He had respected his mother's wishes not to look for him while she was alive, but now he wanted to know the secrets behind why she had forbidden it. I told Michael that if he did want to find his father, I would help him.

Things hadn't changed with my health, and I still did not have much energy, but I was determined to help Michael find his dad. Actually it became more of a job for me; the research was extremely interesting, and it certainly kept my mind off not being well.

Michael had given me the basic information to start out with, like where they had lived when he was born, and that his dad was in the Marines, which pretty much summed up the information I had to go on.

I immediately contacted the Marines, but because of the privacy act, found it nearly impossible to retrieve any information. After several phone calls to the Marines, in several different departments, and even contacting the Church where Michael was baptized, we still didn't even have his social security or military ID number, but trust me, the Marines knew exactly who and where he was, but unfortunately couldn't even tell us whether Mr. Tenaci was dead or alive.

The Marines requested that Michael write a letter addressed to his Dad, send it to them and, "If they find him, they will forward it to him, at which time it would be up to him to respond." This letter was going to end up being the key to Michael's childhood. After all, Mr. Tenaci did leave Michael's mother with, at the time, three toddlers, one of which was Michael.

Once the letter was complete, I forwarded it to the Marines in Quantico, West Virginia, and continued to correspond back and forth with them on the phone, as well as via US mail. It could take months, maybe even years, to find him; all we could do was try.

Day after day, I would check the mail hoping that a letter would arrive from Mr. Tenaci, but it was starting to appear that we would never hear anything from him. Michael continued to work, and I was home everyday raising our girls.

I remember him coming home from a side job one evening, which in construction is referred to as moonlighting. On this particular evening, he reached for his wallet, and realized it wasn't there. His expression went stone cold. So I asked him where he had left it, and he said he left it on the back of his truck. I said, *"Well, that is simple enough, just go back and get it."* His reply was dubious, and he said that he couldn't go back to get it. Then he said, "It probably fell off in the road somewhere anyway."

My gut was telling me that something indecorous was happening, and I didn't like it. What was he up to now, and why was he being so defensive? I asked him where his retainer was, and he replied, "What do you mean?" I said, *"You know what I mean, the one you wear everyday on your teeth!"* He said,

"Oh, I got really sick at work today, and when I threw up it must have gone down the toilet."

My goodness, how coincidental, a wallet, and a retainer? I could feel my blood boiling over, and I knew he was deceiving me. My suspicions told me that his wallet and retainer were probably on someone's nightstand; I had a powerful voice inside of me telling me he was being completely untruthful.

Finally, the letter we had been waiting for arrived from the US Marine Corps. They had located Michael's father! Michael and I were both delighted; the bad news was that they could tell us only that they had located him, and nothing more.

They had forwarded our letter onto him, and now it was up to him to respond. It had been approximately thirty years since he had seen his son, and maybe he didn't want to; maybe he had a family that didn't know about Michael. It was a very precarious situation; however, I prayed for Michael's sake that his father would respond.

Several months had passed and unfortunately, I continued to have an abundance of medical problems. The doctors were still puzzled, and I was now completely lethargic; it was almost as if my muscles had atrophied. I was still having the seizure-type spells, accompanied by extensive bone and joint pain from head to toe. I didn't even have enough energy to hold a cup of coffee.

My health was really diminishing, and I knew there was something seriously wrong with me. You couldn't possibly feel that horrible and be healthy. In addition, Michael, well, what about Michael?

As if we didn't have enough to worry about, Michael's income wasn't the most reliable at that point. Even though he was still with the union, he didn't have a steady contractor to work for, and with all that money in the bank, investments, and a small inheritance, he wasn't exactly motivated to find something more lucrative.

He took integral advantage of the money; we were not independently wealthy, the money was for our house!

Weeks turned into months, and Michael would tell me that he was down at the union hall, but there was no work for him. He had been coming home every day so completely exhausted, and with a sob story about not being able to find a reliable employer. None of this seemed to bother him, and thousands of dollars were being taken out of our savings account. I just couldn't take it anymore! My husband thinking we were independently wealthy, and that he need not find gainful employment! Our relationship had begun to suffer as a result, and we were constantly arguing.

I remember him sitting back in his cozy chair in our living room, without a worry in the world, and I said, *"Get off your ASS and go get a job! What is wrong with you? You have a family to raise here, and many obligations. You can't continue to use our savings account to support us!"*

He just stared at me with those glossy, green eyes, and a very sedate expression. He didn't even say a word; I was screaming at the top of my lungs, yet there was absolutely no response from him. I picked up the portable phone, and hurled it across the room with such anger that it ripped a hole in the wall. By then, I was frothing and still there was absolutely no reaction from him whatsoever. What a jackass! This made me even angrier. I felt as if I were talking to a wax replica of my husband from a museum! That was it! I bent down, and with a closed fist, punched him right in the face. I could hear the sound of his nose crack, and suddenly the wax corpse came to life.

"Oh, my God! I think I broke his nose!" There was blood everywhere. It was the first sign of life I had seen in nearly an hour of heated arguing. He said, "You broke my fricken nose!" I was in shock, and couldn't believe what I had just done.

I didn't know what he had been doing for almost a year, but he hadn't been looking for a job. He rushed out the front door holding his face; I brought him some cold, wet, facecloths, and I said, *"Michael, I am so sorry."*

By now, both of us were crying and I continued, *"Michael, you just pushed me to the limit this time, I don't even know you anymore! You leave early in the morning, come home exhausted, and are a very different person! You don't want to work, and you always have so many deceitful excuses when talking to me lately."*

That had been a hell of a way to get his attention. I hadn't intended to strike him, and I am certainly not a violent person; I guess he just pushed me over the limit and I completely lost it. We took care of his nose without too much of a problem, and it didn't appear to be broken. He promised to get motivated, and find gainful employment to help support his family, instead of using up our entire life savings.

Within a week, he had found himself a job through his union with a contractor that just so happened to be going non-union. We were apprehensive about the change from union to non-union mainly because of the benefits, however, we were reassured by the company's owner that wages and benefits would remain the same, with the exception of having to pay union dues.

It was springtime, and altogether I had been seen at four hospitals, by eleven different specialists. I had had needles, tubes, scans, x-rays, blood work, and diagnostic tests that covered every nook and cranny of my debilitated body. Pain pills, many pain pills to manage the immense amount of pain I was enduring. What I wanted to know was how

they could prescribe pain medications for me when they didn't know what they were treating?
I was so distressed by it all that I just couldn't take it anymore. When the last of the eleven specialists gave me yet another pain pill prescription, I started to cry.

Having lost my composure, I took the prescription, shredded it into a million tiny pieces, and threw it onto the desk at the nurses' station. I said, *"This is what I think of his fricken pain pill prescription!"* I didn't need this; I needed to know what was wrong with me! Didn't anyone believe me?

The nurse knew exactly what I was talking about, and had seen all too well what I had been going through. She told me to try to calm down, and I said, *"No, damnit, this isn't in my head, there is something wrong with me!"* And with that, I walked out and never went back.

My family and I were completely flustered by all of this, and decided to go and see our old family doctor who had retired, and since moved away. He would know what was wrong with me. We drove an exhausting six hours through the mountains of the Sierras, and down into the flatlands of the valley, before reaching his home office in the woods.

Once inside his office he reviewed my scans and diagnostics; he was rather unsettled by the reports as well as with my exam. The results and symptoms were so complex and pointed to several different things. He immediately took notice of one of my eyelids, which was always droopy, and seemed to coincide with a multitude of symptoms I was having. He was extremely puzzled by everything except the eyelids, which was a symptom of dystrophy. He recommended an immediate follow-up evaluation by a neurologist in the North Bay.

I remember stopping at a gas station in Reno, and throwing away all the pain medications that I had from one of my previous prescriptions. My Mom said, "Sara, for Christ sakes, if he doesn't find anything wrong with you then you probably don't have anything wrong with you! Now you have to stop this!"

I was crying hysterically and saying, *"You don't believe me either? My own mother doesn't even believe me."* She got out of the car, and retrieved my medications from the garbage and said, "Sara, what the hell is the matter with you throwing your pain pills away like that? You need them, don't you?"

I said, *"Why do I need them, I'm fricken crazy, right? I'm a nutcase and I just imagined being sick, right? Can't you see how much I am hurting, and how sick I am?"* Mom and I, both very stubborn Italian women, drove for several hours without saying a word to each other.

Driving with tears rolling down my cheeks, I thought to myself, *"I am truly on my own now, maybe I have lost my marbles! How can all this pain and discomfort be in my head? What are my three little girls thinking when they see their Mommy always sick and in pain? What about Michael, does he think I'm nuts too?"*

Finally, mom and I arrived back home after an exhausting and most unpleasant trip. I was so happy to be out of that fricken car, and the best part of being home was getting to hold and love my precious little girls, and be held in Michael's arms. So what if I was crazy, they didn't care; they loved me unconditionally, and I was going to love them just as much too.

36

Life went on, and we were all doing the best we could to enjoy it. One afternoon, the girls were playing in the backyard when suddenly I heard frightful screaming. I ran out to the backyard, half afraid to even see what had happened. Madeline had been stung by a bee, our first bee sting, and as you can imagine, she was very upset.

She was still so tiny, like a petite little bug, which was actually her nickname, "bug." I quickly picked her up, and ran into the house. I couldn't tell where she had been stung because she wasn't just pointing to one area. I sat her up on the sink, and immediately started tearing off her little play clothes. She had obviously been stung more than once.

As Millie and Madison looked on in fear that their little sister was really hurting, I tried to give Madeline Benadryl and Tylenol, while trying to allay their fears as well. I ran a bath for her in the sink, and tried to comfort her as much as possible. Eventually she calmed down and said, "Mommy, I got stung by a bee wearing a yellow jacket!" She was so serious, but we knew that she meant she had been stung by a yellow jacket; it was just too cute, and very amusing.

Valentine's Day that year was very special, Michael and I had been married almost ten years, and I wanted to do something impassioned. So, while he was at work, which ended up being until very late, I cooked some delectable goodies in our kitchen, and warmed up the atmosphere in our bedroom a bit.

The girls were spending the night at Grandma and Grandpa's house, so the evening belonged to just Michael and I. However, he didn't come in until just around midnight, although I wasn't sure why he was so late. But in any case, I had several surprises for him.

Soft, mood music with the lights dimmed down low, and our bedroom decorated in the most romantic fashion. I had placed vivid red, pearly white, and soft petal pink helium-filled balloons around the room, some with Mylar in a heart shape, and others with cupid. I had already slipped into something more comfortable before Michael got home, and had on my deep red, silk robe with matching silk gown underneath.

When Michael came in the door, he could smell the aroma of all the pungent foods I had prepared for us. His facial expression was priceless, and he seemed to be very satisfied with what I was wearing. What he didn't know was that I had purchased some special Valentine boxers for him to wear that night too.

I didn't allow him to go into the kitchen, and while he was getting ready for a nice quiet romantic evening, I brought all the specially prepared appetizers into our bedroom on fine

China, along with two crystal wine glasses, and a bottle of bubbling champagne.

Our little romantic interlude was about to unfold with the two of us sharing an impassioned evening together. I put several dozen bright red, heart-shaped, helium-filled balloons under our bedcovers, and made sure that Michael pulled the covers back.

As he pulled them back, he was delighted to see all the tiny little hearts floating slowly over our bed toward the ceiling. We didn't really need the champagne or the helium to be floating into the heavens; we had already found heaven wrapped up in each other's arms, with a fervent desire to appease each other's wildest fantasies.

37

Almost a year had passed since my very obscure illness began. I was trying to raise my girls, and enjoy all the pleasures that accompany parenthood, although I was often overly-fatigued after little or even no exertion, hurting, and feeling as if my bones were being crushed, my joints on fire. However, I refused to compromise my care and love for my girls; they were my life, and I would move mountains for them. But I did need to find out what was wrong with me.

Finally, I was able to get an appointment at a medical clinic in the North Bay, where I was seen by a neurologist and a rheumatologist. They worked together in running a multitude of diagnostic blood tests on me, and, within less than a week, at long last, I had a diagnosis, which included two life-threatening disorders, both of which all eleven previous doctors had failed to recognize.

I had "Systemic Lupus Erythematosus," an autoimmune disease affecting my entire body, especially soft tissue, and all major organs, as well as one of the dystrophies, "Myasthenia Gravis," which affects nerve and muscle function. Even though this was difficult to fathom, it was a relief to know that I really was not crazy! For much too long I had been led to believe that this illness was all in my head, and now I could finally get some relief, be treated, and live a normal life. Well, as normal as possible.

Within four months, the doctors had a handle on my diseases, and now wanted to address the mass in my chest, which had been inconclusive in the biopsy the previous year. I would now have to undergo Atherectomy, which was "open heart surgery," because the mass, which needed to be removed, was behind my heart. *"Okay, what is God's plan for me? Is this ever going to end?"*

Since I would soon have surgery, I had to contact our medical insurance provider for authorization. I knew my surgery would cost a minimum of fifty thousand dollars, and was so grateful that we had full coverage; otherwise, I didn't know how all the medical expenses would be taken care of. I called our insurance provider, and spoke with someone in charge of benefits to give her all of the information.

However, the call became a nightmare; I was informed that Michael's employer had stopped paying for all of our coverage, and that this surgery, and all other medical bills were going to have to come out of our own pocket.

My body was at boiling point. There had to be some kind of mistake here, Michael's pay stubs showed the medical insurance deduction every week! The benefits representative said, "No, honey, there is no mistake, you have no insurance coverage for you or anyone in your family." How were we going to pay for all these medical bills?

And how was I going to be able to have surgery now?

By the time Michael got home from work, my emotions had evolved into those of a maniac. I had already called Michael at work to tell him, so that he was aware of the situation, but as usual, he was not nearly as upset about it as I was. I think he was missing the required "upset cells" we all have when things go wrong.

We argued back and forth with each other, as well as with his employer, on the phone. His employer denied ever having had a part in this, swore that he had paid our benefits, and told us not to worry.

Michael continued to work for them, meanwhile I would make several phone calls a day to the state of California, regarding Cobra and ERISA benefits. By then it had become obvious that since Michael's employer was completely aware of my medical problems, he was making every effort to avoid having to pay our medical coverage. After fighting with them for several days about our benefits, they suddenly felt compelled to call Michael at home on a Sunday evening and fire him.

Meanwhile, Michael and I retained an attorney that specialized in Cobra and wrongful termination cases, such as ours. The contractor had committed fraud by taking money for medical benefits and not paying them, had breached his contract with Michael when he didn't honor our complete benefits package, and was also guilty for wrongful termination- firing Michael in an attempt to avoid the entire situation.

So, I was due for surgery, and we had no medical insurance, Michael had just lost his job, and there was no way we were going to meet the capital gains tax deadline and purchase our new home. We had already accumulated several thousand dollars in medical expenses, and I just didn't know what we were going to do!

Let me put this into perspective: a family of five, sitting on top of the world, then suddenly mom gets very sick, accruing several thousand dollars in medical expenses, dad's employer stops paying benefits, dad gets fired... What was the most reasonable solution here? Yes, we had to file for bankruptcy.

We filed for bankruptcy in order to get some relief from the medical expenses; however, we were unable to include the capital gains because they hadn't actually become due yet. So we would have to re-file when they became due.

Since Michael didn't have a job, our savings were diminishing rapidly. In addition, when you file for bankruptcy you have to disclose all your assets, including all savings and investments, which become the property of the bankruptcy court.

Also, we had another major financial issue to deal with, which was that I still needed surgery, and we didn't have any medical insurance. I made several calls to find a company that would cover me, which wouldn't have been a big deal for a healthy person, but for me, with several major, preexisting medical problems, it was a nightmare.

Finally, I did find a company that would give me temporary (high cost) coverage; I called Stanford and they arranged to accept it, and recommended contacting Medicare for the remainder of my expenses. This was totally disheartening to me. I shouldn't have had to do that! We were not poor people. I qualified for Medicare without any hassles, and they were going to take responsibility for my surgery, and the stay at Stanford.

Meanwhile, Michael found himself another job, which was great news. However, since our finances had taken such a hit, we had to move out of the rental house, and into a much smaller, less expensive, two-bedroom condo. The girls found it entertaining to be moving into another home. It would be difficult though; they couldn't take any of their outside playthings, including the swing set, because we wouldn't have a yard.

Preparing for my stay at Stanford was beyond stressful, but all of my family and friends were very supportive; none of us could believe all the adversity we had had to face, and I was not sure what was going on with Michael. He seemed to be preoccupied with his own interests, which didn't include our children and me.

It was November 12, 1991, and I was spending an abundance of quality time with my three little girls; the most precious things in my life. I wanted to share as much love, hugs, and kisses with them as possible before going into surgery. I knew that they were just as afraid as I was, although they were not old enough to understand how serious this was. Nevertheless, they knew how much I loved them, which was more than life itself. Leaving them behind while I went into surgery would be heartbreaking. *"Am I ever going to see my little girls, or any of my family and friends again? What if I don't make it through surgery? There is no way that Michael can raise our girls the way that I can! He is not a mommy, and my girls need their Mommy!"*

My heart was breaking as I said goodbye to everyone; it was as if we were never going to see each other again. Two doctors and a couple of nurses wheeled me down a wide, bright white hallway. Everything seemed to be silent except for the sound of the wheels of my gurney rolling around and around with a slight squeak.

There were doctors and nurses coming and going from every direction, and yet, I felt alone. My tears seemed to flow endlessly down my cheeks. One of my nurses said to me, "It's okay to be afraid, but don't worry, our team of doctors and nurses will take good care of you."

My gurney was now being wheeled into the operating room, and with this, the intensity of my heartbeat was beyond what you could imagine. I was so frightened, and I was crying my eyes out. There must have been a team of twenty doctors and nurses in there with me, all dressed in that dreadful, faded green, surgical attire with the masks covering most of their faces.

As they were preparing me for surgery, tears and all, I was able to see one of the nurses. I was not at all happy with what she was getting ready, which appeared to be the saw they would use to cut through my rib cage, before cracking it open. *"Oh, my gosh, No! I don't want them to do this to me. I am much too afraid!"* As I lay there strapped down on the operating table, I was very non-compliant. I didn't have the use of my arms because there were IV's and all sorts of other things already connected to me.

One of the nurses was comforting me, and at the same time wiping away the tears streaming down my cheeks. I don't think I have ever been more frightened in my life.

My surgeon, cardiologist, and entire team were now ready. The IV's were all in place, all the monitors were beeping and buzzing, and I was still awake enough to hear my doctor. He was telling me not to be alarmed when I woke up because I would be in the Cardiac Intensive Care Unit after surgery. *"Why?"* I asked.

He explained that it was a very serious surgery, that I would be in surgery for at least three hours, and that they would actually be moving my heart to get to the tumor that was growing behind it. They would have to monitor me very closely after the surgery.

That made me even more upset, but before long I could feel my entire body becoming flimsy, and weakening from the anesthesia that was running through my veins. Within seconds, I was unable to move, hardly able to keep my eyes open.

Everything seemed to be getting foggy, almost as if I were in a cloud. I had lost complete control of my body, and couldn't move. I thought that must be what dying felt like, so peaceful, as if I had let go of life.

My tenacious body and mind were desperately trying not to fall asleep, but to no avail. As I felt my body slipping further and further away, the anesthesiologist placed a clear, plastic mask over my face and asked me to relax, and count backwards.

38

"Beep, beep, beep ..." I could hear the sharp sound of all the monitors. The surgery was over with, and I was in the Cardiac Intensive Care Unit. Yes, I was experiencing a great deal of pain, pain that I had never endured before. My vision was quite foggy, and I was unable to speak. I had tubes and needles stuck into almost every orifice of my body. Breathing and chest tubes, IV's, catheters, kidney function monitors, oxygen, EKG equipment... I had never seen so many electronic devices connected to one body.

Barely able to move because of the ten-inch incision in the middle of my chest, and even in my somewhat partial coma state of mind, I realized that my breast was uncovered, and tried desperately to pull the sheet over myself.

I guessed hours had passed by, and I was allowed only one visitor for five minutes every hour. With my big Italian family, you know this is impossible. I can remember my cousin, DeeDee, coming in to see me, and giving me a gentle hug.

Then I remember waking up and seeing Michael standing at the foot of my bed with my best friend, Julia's sister, Jennifer. The two of them were just gabbing away, and hadn't realized that even though I was heavily sedated with morphine, I could see them through my still, glazed eyes. Jennifer was a sweetie and I was happy that she had come to see me. Julia was living in Texas then, but I knew if it weren't for her living out of state she would have been right there by my side.

I remember waking up in the wee hours of the morning, and wanting something to drink, which my nurse helped me with, as well as my malt balls. Julia had sent me a box of malt balls, which were one of our childhood favorites, and she knew it would bring a smile to my face, and bring back good memories.

By the following day, even though still heavily sedated, I was a lot more coherent. I was apprehensive about movement, though, and felt as if I would break with the slightest motion.

My team of doctors came in to talk to me, and tell me how my surgery had gone. I had obviously survived the surgery, but the surgeon proceeded to tell me that the tumor they had removed from behind my heart was enormous, the size of a baseball, and had grown into my thymus gland (which controls the immune system), and wrapped around my phrenic nerve, which controls breathing. This explained the crushing chest pain, as well as the seizure activity. Apparently, it was suffocating me, and had I listened to the other eleven doctors, and gone with their judgment that I was a hypochondriac, I would have in fact died. He said, "This surgery may have been difficult for you, but it saved your life!"

Before moving me to a private room, they had to disconnect all of the bells and whistles, meaning all of the tubes and needles. Everything went pretty well, except the removal of the chest tube; I screamed blue murder when they pulled that one out. It felt as if all of my organs were coming out with it.

Once I was in my private room, I had regular visitor privileges, and, of course, my favorite was seeing my girls and Michael. I had lots of company from family and friends, which certainly helped lift my spirits, knowing how much I was loved. My doctors kept me full of lots of morphine and steroids.

Since our insurance was so frugal, I was only allowed to stay in the hospital for a short period of time, and so even though not up to it, I was released on the fourth day.

My girls were all so happy to have me back home, and I was happy to be home. Michael was working long hours, so I didn't get to see too much of him. My mom and Grandma Chirco were my round-the-clock nurses; I couldn't have done it without them there by my side.

I can remember waking up one evening and finding my Grandma standing over my bed, looking at me, and gently touching me with her delicate, little hands. What was she doing? She was making sure that I was okay, and still breathing. Breathing was good!

Sometimes Michael would help me, but most often he was so exhausted when he came home from work that he would sleep through most of my discomfort. I knew he was tired, but how did he think I felt after undergoing something so traumatic?

Since winter was rolling in, and with it lots of rain, Michael was once again out of a job, due to poor weather conditions. I thought he needed to start looking for another way to make a living, other than construction. Money was becoming tight for us, and Santa was going to have to be extremely frugal that Christmas. As the girls still believed in Santa Claus, we couldn't tell them that Santa was poor that year.

Grandma and Grandpa wouldn't take no for an answer, and insisted on helping us out; Millie got the bicycle she asked Santa for, as well as a letter telling her that while flying through the star bright midnight sky, her helmet fell out of his sleigh, and he was unable to catch it. Of course, she would have to have a helmet before riding her bike, but she actually found that very entertaining, thank goodness. Madeline and Madison found it funny too, even though they really were much too young to understand. Madeline and Madison got their little ride-on toys, and other fun stuff as well.

My godparents were retiring, and moving out of the area. We weren't really happy about that, but the good news was they let us move into their home, and pay the same rent as in the condo. We were all excited about this, especially knowing the girls would again have a yard to play in, ride their bikes, and roller skate, instead of being cooped up in the condo.

The months seemed to fly by, and once again spring was in the air. Michael was still working in construction, although that trade was making us poor, and I thought he should be looking into another profession. I kept wondering when he would come home, and tell me he had been laid off again.

It was a really lovely day, the sun was shining brightly and the birds were chirping... it was very pleasant, and I could see the mailman coming up our walkway to the front door. Typically, he just put the mail into our mailbox and left, but that day, he knocked on our door.

It looked like a certified letter, but who was sending us certified mail? I hoped it wasn't more bad news because we had certainly had our share. I signed for the letter, and turned it over to see who had sent it to us, actually to Michael...

I started to scream, and the mailman must have thought I had lost my marbles. It was from Mr. Tenaci! He was alive; we had found him! Michael was going to be so excited! I couldn't wait for him to get home to see the letter. I couldn't and wouldn't open it; it was from his father, so I would have to wait patiently...

When Michael came in from work, I said, *"Guess what? Look what arrived today!"* He picked up the letter, completely dumbfounded. I was more excited than he was; he was apprehensive, and not even sure if he wanted to open it, or just close that chapter of his life. After all, it had been thirty-two years since he had last seen his father, so they were complete strangers.

I said, *"Michael, you wanted to find your father and we did. We worked so hard to find him so that you could find out what you have been searching your heart and mind for all of these years. The answers might be waiting in this letter. You need to open it."*

So with that in mind, he opened the letter; the two of us were sitting together in the family room as he read the letter aloud. Michael's dad was living at a private school in upstate New York. No, he wasn't a teacher, but a grounds man and maintenance man. He had put his phone number in the letter so that Michael could make contact with him. At first, Michael was nervous and had no idea what he would say; I wasn't even sure he would ever call his dad. I think he was still in shock that we had actually located him, and most of all that his dad had wanted to make contact with him.

39

"Hi, Dad!" Wow, with the exception of my dad, Michael had never said, "Hi, Dad" to anyone until that moment! I didn't know about Michael, but it made me very teary-eyed. I hoped they could get together, and try to build a father-son relationship. Michael and Mr. Tenaci spoke for quite a while and when they were finished, I had a chance to speak with him too. We discussed our girls, his three granddaughters, and tried to catch him up on the rest of his family, including my mother-in-law, his ex-wife, who had passed away.

I tried to encourage Michael to fly to New York to get reacquainted with his dad, but he didn't seem to be interested. So we talked, and agreed that maybe his father could visit us in California for a week. We continued to keep in contact with Mr. Tenaci by phone and US mail; we even sent him goodie packs with cookies and photographs. The girls were excited to know that their Daddy had a Daddy too, and that they had another grandfather.

After a couple of months had passed, during one of my conversations with Mr. Tenaci, it appeared that he had been drinking excessively. He actually voluntarily told me that he had a drinking problem, and was an alcoholic. He also proceeded to tell me what had really happened to him, and why he had left his family over thirty years earlier. He hadn't gone AWOL at all, as

Michael's mother had led him and his siblings to believe. Now we knew why she hadn't wanted Michael to know about his father's whereabouts.

Mr. Tenaci hadn't done anything wrong at all; he was in the Marines when Michael was born, and Michael's mother also worked at the base in Quantico, West Virginia. And one night after returning home from duty, he caught Mrs. Tenaci, Michael's mother, with his best friend; she was having an affair with Michael's dad's best friend!

I couldn't believe that after all these years of Michael and his siblings believing their dad had gone AWOL, and they were forbidden to find him, the truth finally came out... now we knew why it was forbidden; she was the one that had something to hide!

This was when Mr. Tenaci walked out, and started to drink in excess, ultimately becoming an alcoholic. Mrs. Tenaci moved with the kids to New York, and then New Jersey, and onto California, in an attempt to stay away from him, and her own lies. He tried desperately to keep in contact with his children, but she kept running.

He had never remarried or had any other children, and I felt sorry for him being all alone, without his family for all those years. Yes, he did date, but was never able to put his heart into a lasting relationship.

Michael and I sent him a disposable camera, so that he could take some photographs, and then send it back to us to develop. Within about a week we received the camera, and immediately brought it to be developed. We wondered if Michael looked anything like his dad. Was he tall, short? What color were his eyes, his hair? Was he thin or did he have a burly build? We wondered about many things.

As I opened the photographs, I saw something so formidable that I immediately put them back into the envelope, and closed it. My heart was racing. The girls were yelling; they wanted to see the pictures. They were loathsome, and there was no way I could show my girls these photographs. What was he thinking sending this film back to us? There had to be something wrong with him. With whom did he associate? What a creep! There was no way I was going to have him come to California to visit us!

After Michael arrived home and I shared these disgusting photographs with him, he agreed that it was the most repulsive thing anyone could ever have done. What if the girls had seen them before I had a chance to do so? The man had serious psychological problems. Why would anyone in their right mind send photos showing their private parts? And we weren't talking fingers and toes here; we were talking male anatomy!

Michael was completely embarrassed by this, and called his father in disgust. He denied having had anything to do with the photographs, and said that his friends had probably gotten a hold of his camera. If so, what kind of friends did he hang around with, and why were they working at a private school?

Michael told his father that we no longer had any interest in being a part of his life, that it was completely disgusting and unacceptable, and that it would be a cold day in hell before he came to visit us, as there was absolutely no way we would want him around our girls.

Mr. Tenaci pleaded with Michael to believe him, and said that someone must have played a foul trick on him. If so, like I said, who were his friends? Mr. Tenaci continued to write, but Michael did not bother to respond. We even received a call from the Pastor at the Salvation Army, which was the shelter where Mr. Tenaci ended up, and he begged us to give him another chance. He told Michael how sorry he was that this had happened, and to please give him another chance.

Michael said, "Absolutely not. I do not take chances like this, and I have a family here to worry about." This would ultimately put an end to the relationship that had been missing, was found again, and now was gone forever. Michael had decided that was it, he had found out what he needed to know, and that chapter of his life would now be closed forever.

Life went on, and we were hoping things would soon improve for us. The lawsuit we had filed against Michael's employer some time earlier was still going on, and was a real nuisance. It seemed to be taking forever; it was always a complex case, especially when it involved ERISA and Cobra benefits.

The sun was still shining brightly, although the leaves were all turning beautiful browns, oranges, and yellows. There were piles of them on the street everywhere you looked, from the gentle breeze blowing them around.

One afternoon, Grandma came to visit us. I loved it when she came to visit us. I still loved to cuddle and snuggle up next to her, like a teddy bear; she was so squishy and lovable, and her perfume was always so fresh and clean. We saw her about once a week, and the girls were just crazy about her; she spoilt them rotten.

Even though she would soon turn eighty-nine years old, she was as bubbly as a spring chicken; she had no problem getting down on the floor and playing with the kids if they wanted her to. It was precious to watch her with them.

We had had a nice visit but it was now time for Grandma to go home. Once again, there were big hugs, only this time it was a bit different; it was as if we hadn't hugged in years, or maybe as if we were never going to see each other again.

She said, "Babe, take care of yourself!" I said, *"Okay, Grandma, I will, don't worry. I love you..."* And she said, "I love you too!" We let go of each other's embrace, and she left with a big, beautiful smile on her face, that of an angel. I couldn't explain the unusual feeling I had then; I couldn't quite put my finger on it, but I knew I did not like what I was feeling.

A couple of days had passed since Grandma's visit. That evening she was going out to dinner with Auntie Barbara and Uncle Anthony. By the time she got home, she was feeling quite dizzy. I talked to her on the phone, and she said she didn't feel well at all; I thought perhaps her blood pressure medication needed to be adjusted. I wanted her to rest so I said, *"Grandma, I love you,"* as I always would tell her, and then I said, *"I hope you feel better by morning."* Grandma said, "I love you too, babe..."

40

I could hear something, but I wasn't sure if I was dreaming or not, what was that startling sound? It sounded like our telephone ringing. It couldn't be... it was too early for anyone to be calling, and everyone was still sleeping. I answered it. *"Hello?"* I could hear someone screaming hysterically on the line. "She's not breathing! I can't get her to breathe!"

My heart was beating out of control, and I just couldn't believe what I was hearing; it was my aunt calling to say that Grandma had stopped breathing. I said, *"Calm down, please try to calm down, and tell me what happened? Are you sure? Dial 911! We will get there as soon as we can."* Our precious little Grandma had fallen into a deep sleep, and I knew that she had probably passed away.

Michael was now awake, and there I was trying to be this mountain of strength with my Mom right across the hallway yelling, "What's the matter, is Grandma all right?" Mom was staying with us for the week while my Dad and brother were fishing. So, never having had to deal with anything so emotionally painful, I didn't know what to do or say.

I said, *"I don't think she is feeling very good, we have to hurry up and go over there, auntie and uncle dialed 911."* I didn't know what to do, and my mom was screaming hysterically, because, like me, she realized that something dreadful had just happened. I was thinking, *"Dear God, please give me the strength to do this!"*

Michael stayed home with the girls, so that Mom and I could race over to Grandma's house. Meanwhile, I called my Dad and brother in San Diego, and they headed home. Since Mom was in quite an emotional state, I helped her into the car; the ride seemed to take hours, although I knew that we only lived ten minutes away.

At every red light, Mom would scream more for me to hurry. As we turned the corner onto Grandma's street, the paramedics and fire department had already made it inside. Oh, my God, this was it, what did I do now? Mom was yelling, "Sara, did Grandma die, did she die?" *"Yes, Mom, Grandma died,"* I said.

I could no longer hold my composure. Mom was ready to jump out of the car, at which time the paramedics could see how distraught she was, and came over to take care of her as well.

While Mom was on the porch receiving oxygen, I ran into Grandma's house where the air was still and somber. A couple of my aunts and uncles were already there, including the two that lived with Grandma. The tears could have filled an ocean.

I thought of that day when Grandma had hugged and kissed me as if we were never going to see each other again; she must have known then that she would soon be going to heaven.

I slowly drifted into her room as if in the fog of a bad dream. I could see her lying peacefully in her bed, sleeping like an angel. I bent down at her bedside, and gently touched her silky smooth face, giving her a hug and kiss. I was not afraid to touch her. I loved her so much! Why had this happened? She wasn't ready to go yet!

The next several days were very traumatic for all of us. When you love someone so much, you don't ever want to think that they could be taken away from you. To all of us, Grandma was invincible and nothing could ever harm her or take her away.

But the reality was that Grandma had had a stroke, and died in her sleep. She would no longer be with us to share in all the love and joy she brought into our lives. Within a short three-day period, we had all the services, including the wake, rosary, and funeral. It was heartbreaking, to say the least, and not a dry eye could be found. Even in death, she was still beautiful. A beautiful person from within as well. Everyone who knew her loved her. We all had so many wonderful memories of her that we would always hold dear to our hearts.

41

Michael and I were still struggling with our finances, and he still didn't seem to comprehend that he needed to be gainfully employed. Our groceries were dwindling, and our meals were becoming limited. It was difficult to explain to the girls what was happening. I didn't want to ask my parents for help either, although without my parents and brother, the kids would definitely have been hungry.

For Michael, it seemed that he knew that if we needed help, my family would always be there, and that was just too easy. He was an adult and needed to find a real job to support his family.

With the exception of the small disability social security check I was receiving, I was unable to help much with the finances. Eventually even Michael's unemployment benefits ran out leaving us below the poverty level. Welfare and food stamps! Oh, my God! This was completely humiliating to me. That type of assistance was for poor people, we couldn't be poor! In a three-year period, we had gone from "riches to rags" not "rags to riches." Our lives were completely turned upside down, and Michael still didn't have a clue.

Everyday, Michael still came home exhausted, and crying about how tired he was, and how hard he was looking for another job. I was still wondering where he was really putting all his energy. I couldn't believe that we were now actually down to counting our change, and had three children to feed and take care of. Well, not only food, what about Tylenol? Well, that was exactly what happened. Madeline got sick with a temperature of 103 degrees.

She was so sick, and I tried everything to bring her fever down, including a cold bath, which would make anyone scream. She was burning up, and we had fifty-six cents to our name; I was in tears. How had this happened to us?

Once again, Grandma came to the rescue with Tylenol, and a few dollars to hold us over until our next welfare check came in. With lots of love, Tylenol, cold baths, and alcohol rubs, Madeline's temperature finally started to come down.

Michael was doing small odd jobs but we were still barely making ends meet. The girls were wonderful throughout all of it, even though I was sure they didn't really understand.

The holidays were coming up once again, and the girls wanted to see "Christmas in the Park." The one slight problem was that we didn't have extra money to actually walk them through the park; we knew that if they wanted cotton candy we were not going to be able to buy it for them.

So we decided that we would still enjoy the magic of the Christmas spirit, and we drove them around the park in our van. Everything was so beautiful with all the festive holiday decorations, and thousands of colorful lights shining brightly.

We all enjoyed this, especially the girls. I knew in my heart they would have loved to have gotten out of our van, and parade around with the other children taking pictures with Santa, buying little holiday trinkets to play with, and eating some of the yummy treats. They were wonderful, though, and very excited with what they were able to see from our van.

It was time for a New Year's resolution, and mine was quite simple, and had to do with Michael. We were still on welfare so there was no negotiating my decision.

I said, *"Michael, you have one month to get your act together, and find a real job with full benefits for your family. We have been married for several years now, and we are on welfare and food stamps! This is not acceptable. I will not raise my girls this way. So, find a new way to make a living, because all you are doing right now is coming home tired and with no paycheck. If you don't find one, I'm going to kick your butt out."*

Michael said, "How can I do that?" I said, *"Well, you'd better do it, or I want a divorce. You don't want to go to school. Your excuse is you want to be home with your family, but the truth is even with you not working you are never here with your family! So, what is that all about?"*

Almost one month to the day that I gave Michael an ultimatum, we got a phone call from a Biotech firm that had interviewed him three times for a senior maintenance painting position. He was now being offered the job with full benefits, starting immediately. This was really a godsend.

Finally, after all the hardship including welfare, food stamps, and social security, he was going to have stable employment, with a full benefits package, and a regular paycheck, not something from the state, and job security. I guess putting a fire under Michael's butt did the trick. This was the best news we had had in a long time, and I was proud of Michael for coming through for us.

The stressful lifestyle that I had been so uncomfortable with seemed to be behind us. One morning, I had just dropped Millie and Madeline off at school for the day, and was just going to futz around the house, maybe take Madison for a burger later on in the day.

At about eight thirty a.m. the phone rang, which was very typical. I picked it up thinking it was Grandma, so the strange voice on the other end of the phone startled me. They said, "Mrs. Tenaci?" I said, *"Yes, this is she, who is this?"* She said, "This is Nurse Johnson from the Peninsula Hospital, your husband has been in a terrible accident." I started shaking, and felt as if my blood had been drained out of my body, like so many times before.

She said, "I need you to come down right away." *"Oh, my God!"* I screamed. *"Is he going to be okay?*

Did Michael die?" Oh, my God, I thought they wanted me to come down and identify his body! *"Oh, no, please don't let this be happening to us,"* I thought.

42

The nurse said, "He is quite banged up, but we think he's going to be okay." You need to come and pick him up. *"Oh, thank God! For a moment I thought that I was going to be a widow,"* I said. I called my Mom to watch Madison for me so that I could drive to the hospital.

When I got there, I went over to Michael's bed, and gave him a big hug. He was having a lot of discomfort. His doctor was in the room with us, and told me that the seat belt had saved Michael's life. The truck had been hit broadside on the freeway, and pushed off an embankment, where it then rolled. Michael must have really had an angel on his shoulder that day.

He probably should have stayed out of work for a couple of weeks at least, but since he didn't want to jeopardize his new job, he went back within a couple of days. It didn't take long for him to recuperate, and for things to get back to normal.

Several months had gone by, and we wanted to take the girls on a well-deserved mini vacation down to Southern California. Our little girls were really growing up right before our eyes. Millie was almost eleven, Madeline was six, and Madison was four. We drove, and took a friend along that did some babysitting for us. It did our hearts good to see the girls having the time of their lives in Disneyland. We even had breakfast with the characters. I thought Madison was going to climb right back inside me when they came over to our table, and Madeline, well she got down under the table faster than anyone I have ever seen.

Millie was an old pro, after all she had been there when she was four years old too. She was personality plus with all the characters, and had no problem carrying on a conversation with them, while trying to encourage her two little sisters to do the same.

However, Madeline and Madison were terrified at these larger-than-life characters. Even though they were frightened, the whole situation was just adorable, and within a few minutes, they warmed up to the characters just a tiny bit.

My cousin, Olivia, and her three sons also came with us. So, between all of us, we had lots of fun. We also took a day trip over to Universal Studios, which was unbelievable. I do think the adults had more fun there than the kids did though. After three days, we had all had our fill of amusement parks, and headed back home.

It would be nice if everyday were like a fantasy but it was now time to get back to the basics of everyday living.

Those old haunting capital gains totaling sixty thousand dollars were now due and payable, and as recommended by our attorney we re-filed for bankruptcy; we re-filed chapter thirteen, which would be taken out of Michael's paycheck for five years.

The other thorn in our side was the pending litigation from when Michael's boss had stopped paying our medical benefits, and then fired him. It seemed like it was taking forever. Nothing was ever easy though; our original attorney on the case had committed malpractice by not providing the courts with the pertinent documentation, which was completely detrimental to our case. It was almost like starting at square one, and having to go through an appellate process to get our case back on track.

Our new appellate attorney had his own practice but formerly had a very prestigious position working with a judge on the Supreme Court. We still didn't have tons of money, so he allowed me to work off part of his fees by doing some paralegal work for him. It was very interesting work, in that I had a chance to summarize several court documents for him, including high profile appeals for murder trials. In fact, I was offered a job with the district attorney's office, but kindly refused. Although it was extremely interesting work, I didn't want to be wrapped up working on murder cases; it wasn't upbeat enough for me.

Mr. Michael's, our appellate attorney, was convinced beyond any doubt that our first attorney's behavior had thoroughly jeopardized our chances for a favorable outcome. We tried everything at the ninth district court level to get this overturned to go back and have pertinent documentation and proof of the illegal dealings of Michael's former employer allowed as evidence, but were knocked down every time.

Our only chance was to submit the case to the Supreme Court. We had all the documentation to prove our case, as well as our attorney's negligence in the handling of it. It had become a nightmare to deal with, and I was the only one dealing with it. If I had had to drop it into Michael's lap, and tell him to handle it, he wouldn't have known where to begin.

He had left it completely in my hands, as with almost everything in our lives. Michael thought because he went to work that he shouldn't have to deal with anything else in life.

Mr. Michael's had prepared the Petition with all pertinent legal documentation, and forwarded it to the US Supreme Court. This would be our last chance to get the lower courts to overturn the decision, and allow prominent and detailed information on our behalf back into the litigation.

We had all the facts supporting the employer's misconduct and illegal dealings, which caused us significant damages, but without these facts being submitted by our original attorney, we had very little chance of winning our case. If the Supreme Court would not allow the lower courts to overturn the ruling, we had been advised by our attorney to file a malpractice suit against the original attorney.

This case had drained me, mentally as well as physically. I prayed that the Supreme Court would overturn the ruling, and let us go forward, but we had to wait several weeks to hear from Washington DC.

We received a letter, which stated, "Dear Sir, we regret to inform you that your Petition to the Supreme Court to have the lower courts decision overturned has been denied. Our decision was based solely on the fact that pertinent information to support your case was not documented or submitted at the lower court level by your attorney."

I was overwhelmed by all of this, having worked diligently on the case with Mr. Michael's for over two years. This was not fair. This wasn't justice! When Michael came home from work, I told him that we had received the letter from Washington D.C., and that our petition had been denied.

As usual, Michael said, "Oh, that's not good." However, being the stubborn Italian woman that I was, I would not let them get away with it, and would now pursue it as a malpractice suit, as our appellate attorney had recommended.

Our new malpractice attorney was like a psycho, and had some very strange behavior, but he was supposed to be a shark when it came to litigating malpractice suits. Although it came with a five thousand dollar price tag as a retainer. After meeting with us on several occasions, and having reviewed our entire case, Mr. Jackson came up with a figure for damages in the range of eight hundred thousand dollars, which would encompass all damages. It was in his hands now; we had done everything possible, and had run up against unlimited obstacles. I just hoped that he could use his shark skills where needed.

My aunt and uncle had decided to sell the house we were renting from them, which meant we had to find another rental. It took us about two weeks but we were able to find one within the same school district, which was so important. So ten days before Christmas we moved. I had never seen a decorated tree being moved before, but with great caution, that was exactly what we had to do.

We unplugged our decorated tree, and as if carrying fine China, placed it into the moving van. Our girls were upset that we were moving, but I was sure once we were settled into the new house, they would be just fine. I was sure our puppies, Bambi and Muffin, were also starting to feel like gypsies.

Despite the unusual circumstances we had all had to endure, our little girls were growing into wonderful, well-balanced children, and I just couldn't imagine life without them. That year seemed pretty normal when compared with several previous rocky ones we'd had.

Well, with the exception of Michael and I that is; we seemed to be having quite a few disagreements. I couldn't believe that we had been married for fourteen years already; many couples would have gone their separate ways by then, with all the unfortunate things we had had to endure in our marriage.

All of these stressful situations had certainly taken a toll on me mentally as well as physically; the body and mind can only take so much. One afternoon, while the girls were at school, I went over to Mom and Dad's for lunch.

While sitting at the table, my body suddenly had the most extraordinary sensation. I was starting to tremble as if I was coming apart at the seams. I still had a bite of my turkey sandwich in my mouth, which I could no longer chew. I was losing control; my mind felt as if it was in fast forward, my body wanted to move in all different directions at once, and yet, I couldn't speak. I started to cry. I could hear my Mom saying, "What's the matter? Are you okay? I said, *"No, there is something wrong with me; I don't feel very well."*

I was completely aware of my surroundings, but felt like I was losing control of my body. Mom managed to walk me over to the couch, and lay me down. I was trembling so badly that she literally had to wrap herself around me to try to hold me still.

I was screaming, and my entire body felt spastic. I was scared to death. Was this what a nervous breakdown felt like? Mom was no doubt in a state of panic. Our friend and bookkeeper for my Dad's business, Judy, happened to be there, and had to try to hold onto me, while Mom called the doctor. I felt as if I had lost my mind. Everything was going so fast and I couldn't stop shaking. What was wrong with me?

My doctor's office thought maybe I was having a breakdown, and wanted to see me right away. One slight problem was that Mom couldn't get me off the couch, and I couldn't get up and walk. They suggested we call 911, but I didn't want to do that either. So in an attempt to calm me down, the doctor's office ordered tranquilizers from the pharmacy, hoping they would calm me down enough to be able to come into the office.

I guessed this was how my body was dealing with all the stress it had endured over the previous several years. I was put on Valium for a couple of weeks, in an attempt to get me to relax a bit, and it seemed to be very effective. I didn't like taking medications, or drugs of any type for that matter, so after a couple of weeks of being back to normal, I stopped taking the pills.

Michael seemed to be getting lots of side work, or at least that was the reason he gave me for coming home late from work most nights. I always had his dinner "fit for a king" set aside for him. No matter how late it was, I would always warm his meal, butter his bread, and serve him. Was he spoilt or what?

I wasn't sure what Michael's problem was, as he had been acting strangely for a long time, although with his history of dishonesty, I didn't even want to guess what he might be up to. It seemed we were constantly arguing, which I tried to avoid, especially when the girls were around.

If I asked him where he had been, or why he was coming home so late, he got very defensive, and made all kinds of excuses. He always made a scene in front of the girls, and made it look like Mommy was the asshole for yelling at poor Daddy, when all he was trying to do was work hard to make a living for us.

Millie knew better, but Madeline and Madison idolized Daddy, so, in their eyes, he couldn't do any wrong. Michael knew that and took advantage of it every chance he could.

The girls were doing some modeling, and Madeline had been chosen as one of the children in a Merry-go-round scene at Pier 39 in San Francisco. It was a doggie movie called *Homeward Bound II*. There really weren't any speaking parts for this segment of the movie because the camera focused primarily on the animals. Madeline and I spent an entire day filming at the pier, and had a wonderful time. I knew her favorite thing was getting to be with the dogs and cats. Millie was doing runway modeling, and Madison was afraid of all the camera action, and wasn't interested.

It was hard to believe that it was already 1996. I think my body was still wiped out from the years of stressful situations, and all the disease processes I had had to deal with. I still did not feel very well, and had a strange rash on my tummy. I wondered if my doctor could prescribe a stronger vitamin for me. It kind of looked like shingles, so I decided to monitor it, as well as applying a topical antibiotic to see if that would clear it up. I really didn't feel very well at all.

The girls would soon be joining a community swim program, and if they liked it, would get to swim six days a week. Unfortunately, within the first week of swim team, Millie developed very unusual spots or pimple-like bumps on her back, and within a day or so, her entire body was covered with them.

Millie had chicken pox at fourteen years old, and was very sick with a fever of over one hundred and three degrees, as well as Strep Throat. There was no doubt that Madeline and Madison were exposed to it, and would get it as well.

Within less than three weeks, all three of our girls had gotten the chicken pox, and were all feeling miserable. I gave them all many oatmeal baths to soothe the itching; I thought they were going to itch their skin right off their little bodies. Once they were all feeling better we were able to bring them back to the community pool to join the rest of their swim team friends.

I was so glad the girls were finally over their chicken pox, and wished that I could also start to feel better; I was tired of this not feeling well stuff. When I went to bed at night, it felt as if someone was holding their hand over my windpipe. It was frightening, and extremely uncomfortable. *"Maybe it is just stress,"* I thought. Perhaps if I slept on my side I wouldn't feel like I was suffocating. I just wanted to feel better.

A couple of weeks had passed and no matter which way I slept, I still felt pressure over my windpipe, and I also felt completely lethargic. I went in to see my doctor, he carefully examined my neck, and did some lab work. I didn't like the look on his face, and wondered what he was thinking. He said, "I would like to send you for an ultrasound, and maybe an MRI." *"Okay."* I said. *"But I'm curious, what for?"*

43

It was hard to believe that we were well into February; actually the month had just about ended, as it was the twenty-eighth. While driving to pick up my girls from school, I heard on the news that there was a terrible accident on Highway 85, just a few miles from where I was. They asked all drivers to avoid this area to allow for emergency vehicles. Chills went up and down my spine, and I didn't like the feeling I was having. I prayed that whoever was involved, was not too badly injured.

Unfortunately, within a few hours, we received some heartbreaking news. Our good friend, Rhonda's sister, Carol, was tragically killed in a head-on collision with a drunk driver, whose speed exceeded ninety miles per hour. Suddenly those feelings that chilled my entire body were real; it was not just a bad feeling, but also a living nightmare! Why did things like that have to happen?

Carol would have turned thirty-eight a month after her death, and was survived by her teenage daughter and son. She was such a wonderful, young woman with everything to live for. It was tragic that her life should have ended so abruptly. My heart went out to her family; I didn't think any of them would ever be the same. This was Rhonda's sister, and her best friend. I didn't know how she was going to be able to deal with such a tragic loss. I would pray for all of them with hopes the good Lord would watch over her, and her family.

44

Within a few months, my body that was already so plagued with disease processes had another mountain to climb. After having more diagnostics done on my neck, they found that I had a mass on my thyroid, which would have to be removed. He wouldn't know what kind of mass it was until after I had had the surgery and a biopsy. The girls would be getting out of school in a couple of weeks for summer vacation, so I would wait until then to have the surgery.

Discussing this with my girls was heartbreaking; I had to try to believe that everything was going to be all right, even though I wasn't sure myself. How could I not alarm the girls when I was so frightened myself? Sitting down with my now fifteen, nine, and seven year olds was a real tearjerker. The big question was, "Mommy, are you going to die?"

"No, Mommy is not going to die," I reassured them. *"She will always be here for you."* Then I thought to myself, *"What if I do die?"* My girls are going to think that I lied to them! My family and friends were wonderful throughout all of this. I had lots of love and support, and I tried to use my inner strength to believe that everything was going to be just fine.

I will never forget this as long as I live; it was the night before my surgery, and my nerves were crumbling. I had finally fallen asleep when I was awoken in the wee hours of the morning. I was too tired to open my eyes, or even move, but I felt a presence next to my bed. I was not afraid; it was a peaceful presence.

Upon opening my eyes, there she was, larger than life! I knew it wasn't a dream, and as I desperately tried to focus, I realized it was Grandma. She was standing over me, like an angel, with such beauty and such serenity; I felt as if a spell had been cast on me. With her arms outstretched, she said, "Are you ready to come with me now?" I said, *"No, Grandma, I'm not ready..."* And in the blink of an eye, her presence seemed to fade away like a heavenly fog.

Oh, my God, it wasn't Grandma that scared me; she was a pure, heavenly vision. What scared me was that maybe she was trying to tell me something? Was I going to die? This was not a dream, and if I had ever doubted that our loved ones watch over us after they pass on, I surely didn't doubt it after that. I couldn't tell anyone about this until after the surgery; it would really have frightened them, and they would also think it was some kind of message.

Within a couple of days, my surgery had come and gone, my surgeon having removed one side of my thyroid that had a tumor growing on it. He seemed to think there was nothing to worry about, but I had a little nagging feeling in my gut telling me that something was wrong.

Several more days would pass, and with that came a silent nervous breakdown; the anticipation of the still-unknown biopsy results was haunting me. Six, seven, eight days had gone by, and still no word on the results. I was trying to believe in the "no news is good news" adage, but I couldn't. I would wait one more day before calling my doctor.

Millie, Madeline, and Madison were all busy with swim team, and had become little fish. They were really happy that summer had arrived, Millie had made some new friends, and her best friend, Jolie, was on the swim team with her too. When Jolie was over, it was like having another daughter in the house. Madeline and Madison were also making new friends. It was really important to me that my health didn't interfere with my girls enjoying their childhood; I didn't want to be consumed by it.

It was the 26th day of June 1996, nine days since my surgery, and still no word on the biopsy. I couldn't believe that it was taking so long! I had to call; I couldn't take it anymore! I was taking the girls to see *The Hunchback of Notre Dame* that afternoon, but first I was calling my doctor.

I was pacing back and forth, with an awful feeling inside of me that the news was not going to be good. I wanted to know the results but I was afraid to hear them. What was I going to do if they said the tumor was malignant?

As I sat down in my recliner, I took a deep breath and tried to calm myself down a bit before calling. When the nurse came on the phone, I said, *"I would like to know if my pathology report is in yet? It has been nine days, what seems to be the problem?"* She said, "Oh, hi, Sara. Your biopsy results just came in, can you hold?"

My body was trembling, and I didn't know whether or not I could handle the news, but I just knew that it would be bad. As I rocked back and forth in my recliner, holding the phone to my ear, and waiting for the nurse to come back on the line, I saw my girls sitting in the family room, waiting for Mommy to finish her phone call so that we could go to the movies. It felt as if she had kept me on hold for hours when in reality it was probably only a couple of minutes. "Sara?" *"Yes...?"* "I have your biopsy results."

45

I could feel my body, as it wanted to thrash about wildly with the news. I was screaming, *"Oh, my God, there must be a mistake. I can't have cancer! Dear Lord, please give me the strength I need to get through this."* I was trembling; I didn't know what to do? I hung up the phone, and tried desperately not to make it obvious to my girls that something was wrong.

I made a mad dash down the hall, and into the bathroom, where I drenched my face with cold water. I was talking to myself, and trying to keep it together. I couldn't tell the girls just yet, I just couldn't. I wanted to throw up, I wanted to scream, but I couldn't. I had known it from the feeling that I had in my tummy that it was going to be bad news. I kept telling myself to take deep breaths, relax, and look at your girls...

Suddenly, I felt like I was in a tenebrous twilight zone; I had to pull myself together, and hope the girls didn't notice anything. I wasn't ready to tell them yet. They were waiting anxiously to go to the movies. I was hoping the movie would be distraction enough for me to not think about the horrible news for a while. I just wanted to go and have fun with my girls, and not think about the obvious.

The movie was adorable, the girls were focused on the big screen, and their enormous buckets of hot-buttered popcorn, red licorice, and sodas, just as it should be for a child- not a worry in the world, just a fun day at the movies. I was looking at the big screen too; but I couldn't even tell you what took place in the movie.

Everything was one big blur, and all I kept thinking was, *"I have cancer, me, cancer! What am I going to do?"* Of course my girls had no idea that Mommy had tears rolling down her cheeks, and was wondering if she would be around to enjoy fun times like that one with them, and watch them grow up.

I wanted to be there for them through all the laughter and tears; no one could take care of them and love them the way I did! I wanted to see them go to college, walk down the aisle and get married, have children. I wanted to have grandchildren. I didn't want to miss any of those precious things!

I wouldn't allow it to be taken away from me, or me to be taken away from them. I needed them and they needed me. So, in a couple of hours many things had flashed in front of me, and I honestly couldn't remember anything about the movie except its name, *The Hunchback of Notre Dame*.

The movie ended, the girls having had a fun time; Madison's favorite part of going to the movies was the popcorn, it was finger-licking good for her, and she didn't stop crunching on it until every buttery popped kernel was gone. We went home, and I tried to act as if everything were normal. I hadn't spoken with Michael about it yet, and decided to call him at work.

I said, *"Michael, I found out today that I have cancer,"* and his reaction was no different from the traditional reaction from him. He said, "You're kidding me, that's not good." It had little or no impact on him whatsoever. I felt as if I had just told him that I had a cold. Another day would pass before I decided to tell the rest of my family that the pathology report had come in, and that the tumor was malignant. As one would expect, everyone was overwhelmed with emotion.

Within the next few months, I was seen by an oncologist, surgeon, and several other specialists. I had to undergo another surgery to remove the other side of my thyroid gland, which was still producing cancer cells, and I was given a suppressive hormone treatment to fight any remaining cancer cells.

This cancer had many cell types, and was not encapsulated; it had broken off into my bloodstream, and had what they told me was lymphatic and vascular invasion, which in English meant that it could show up anywhere in my body.

I had a tremendous amount of support from all my family and friends. One of my good friends, Lorraine, and her husband helped me research some information on the Internet on rare and combined cancer cells, and doctors that specifically deal with these. We found a doctor in Rhode Island, who was very helpful in the course of my treatment and recommendations.

Our entire summer seemed to be consumed with my cancer scenario. However, I did not compromise the care of my girls, and made sure that they enjoyed their summer as much as possible. Being diagnosed with cancer changes your life and everything about it; it's never out of your mind. You always have that fear that it will come back.

Stress never seemed to cease in our family; the malpractice attorney we hired to take care of the problems our first attorney created was not doing his job. He allowed all the deadlines for the court-required documentation to expire.

His behavior was bizarre; almost as if he had two personalities. I was starting to think that the lawsuit had been given the evil eye, and was definitely beyond anything in Murphy's Law. Whatever could have gone wrong did. We had an estimated eight hundred thousand dollar lawsuit hanging in the balance, and our attorney had lost his marbles.

His behavior was totally unethical, and inappropriate. He had become verbally abusive, and was like a devil in disguise. Would we ever be finished with this? What could possibly happen next in this lawsuit?

One morning I got a call from the District Attorney's office. As a courtesy, they were calling all our attorney's clients to inform them that he had suffered a massive stroke, and would no longer be able to practice law.

We were given an address of where to go to pick up several boxes of consequential documents, but what good were they without an attorney? According to the courts, the statute of limitations had almost run out. I felt bad that he had had a stroke, yet I just couldn't believe this was happening.

He had made a total mess of everything, and no one was going to want to close the case for us now. Within a couple of weeks, we had hired an independent attorney to put some closure on this case, unfortunately with little avail. The statutes had run out by then, and we went from a six-figure lawsuit to a five-figure one.

It was time to move forward. The most important thing was that I had three beautiful daughters, and my cancer seemed to be stable; none of this could be measured by dollar signs. It was already 1997, and Michael and I were having more than our fair share of difficulties; he was coming home late every single evening, and definitely held the record for the most preposterous excuses.

I personally felt he was having an affair, but we may as well forget him admitting to having one. He came home exhausted every evening with the guiltiest look on his face, ate a dinner fit for a king, then lay down on the floor in the family room, and went to sleep.

I had to confront him, because I could feel it in my heart, and I knew that he was up to no good; it's just something a wife comes to know. There was something ripping my guts out, and I was determined to find out what it was.

Michael always had to put on a show in front of our girls. He tried to make them think he was a saint, and that I was nuts.

During several heated arguments, he always made it a point to say loud enough so that the girls could hear, "You know that I've never been with anyone other than you! You always think I'm cheating on you, or that I'm with someone else. All I do is work my fricken ass off, and come home to you and the girls!" Yeah, he was working his fricken ass off all right, but I honestly didn't think it was on the job!

Going out for coffee with a couple of my good friends, Rhonda and Lorraine, was always fun. We would always have such interesting conversations while enjoying our coffee. Especially when we discussed Michael's unusual behavior. Some of our conversations were heavy, and others were quite humorous.

Neither of them was quite sure what to make of Michael's behavior because they didn't know him well enough to make that judgment, although they hoped for mine and my girls' sakes, that I was wrong in my feeling that he was having an affair.

46

Millie had found herself another new friend on the swim team, and was becoming quite fond of Michelle; Michelle was an only child, and Millie had become her adopted big sister. Michelle fitted right in with our clan, and her parents, Donna and Mike, were wonderful people too. During swim season, you could always find us sitting on the deck of the pool chitchatting, and watching all of our girls swim like fish. Michelle was an awesome swimmer, and wanted to go to the Olympics someday.

I remember one particular evening just like it was yesterday; Michael and I had gotten into yet another argument about his coming home late from work. It was a fiery argument, and I decided to confront him directly about his whereabouts.

The feeling in my gut was dreadful, and was tearing me apart. I had never had a stronger feeling than that that he was up to no good. In many ways, it was so obvious; he had become so distant, and it was as if he were living on another planet. What about our bedroom? Well, that's obvious too. Once you are with a person for so many years, and they suddenly become a different partner and change your lovemaking as if you are another person, you just know it...

When we were intimate, even though he was with me, he wasn't really with me, if you know what I mean? I didn't know where he was getting this new form of romance or intimacy, but it wasn't from me, and I was certain that he was up to no good.

So to get back to our argument, Michael and I were alone in our bedroom, and I flat out told him that I thought he was cheating on me. There we were standing next to our closet doors face-to-face, and in a rage.

His response was that of a loving bastard; he came nose-to-nose with me and screamed as loud as he could, so that once again the girls could hear him from the other side of the house. He said, "I am sick and tired of you always accusing me of being with someone else and cheating on you! All I do is bust my ass, and I have to come home from work and be accused of being with another woman!"

I said, *"Michael, you are a fricken liar!"* He looked me straight in the eyes with a fiery stare and spat right in my face! I couldn't believe it! I was in such a state of disbelief, and devastated by his repulsive actions.

I had had quite enough; what little respect I did have for him was gone after that. My face was soaked from my tears and his spit, and you just can't imagine how this made me feel. In our culture, when you spit on someone, it's like saying they are dirt, or wishing them dead. I was now truly convinced that I had married an asshole.

The girls were always asking me why their Daddy, whom they loved so much, and Mommy were always arguing. Of course they were much too young to understand or sense that something was wrong. Well, with the exception of Millie; Millie, like me, had suspected something for a long time, and really didn't care too much for his behavior.

It would be several days before Michael and I were actually able to carry on a somewhat civil conversation. After having my face spat on, I was not even sure how I could have any conversation with my so-called husband at all.

Nothing had really changed between us, and our marriage was going down the tubes. I continued to do what I typically did, and that was take care of my girls, cook, clean, and just do all of the things a good mommy and wife would enjoy doing.

My best friend, Julia, was in town from the Midwest, and her and her daughter, Katie, came to visit us. They were at our house one afternoon when Michael came in from work. As usual, Michael gave Julia a big kiss on the lips, but when he saw little Katie it seemed as if the world had stopped turning. The air suddenly became very thick-bodied. What was up with this? Michael usually loved children, but that day it was as if he had seen a ghost. I couldn't quite put my finger on it and not sure, I wanted to know what was up with the situation.

Something very strange was happening; Julia seemed fine. It was just Michael, and the presence of the baby, which seemed to be vexing some kind of feelings in him.

Mom also happened to be visiting, and she was like Julia's second mother. It came as no surprise that she just loved little Katie; while smothering her with hugs and kisses, she couldn't seem to take her eyes off her. Was I crazy or did everyone else in this room know something that I didn't?

Later that day, after Julia had left, and Michael was out doing God only knows what, Mom decided that she had something to discuss with me. I didn't like the sound of her voice, or the look in her eyes.

As Mom and I sat down at my kitchen table to have a cup of coffee, I knew she had something to share with me that I wasn't going to like. She seemed perplexed. She said, "Sara, I just cannot believe how much Katie looks like Millie!" I said, *"My Millie?"* She said, "Did you see her eyes? She has Millie's big, beautiful, brown eyes. I just cannot believe the resemblance!" I didn't want to acknowledge what she was saying, but I knew it was true; Katie didn't look anything like her brother. I shouted, *"No!"*

We discussed it further, and I told her it had to have been a coincidence. Wouldn't that just take the cake? That was all I needed.

The conversation with my Mom just added fuel to the fire of what I was already thinking about Michael. She was obviously thinking that Michael was Katie's father, although she had no idea about what had been going on between us, and I didn't plan to share it with her. Besides, Julia lived in Texas, so how could that have happened?

Even though it was a preposterous thought, Julia and Jonathan were having marital problems at the time Katie was conceived, and if memory serves me right, were not even sleeping together. Okay, so how did this happen? How did she get pregnant? I thought that perhaps I shouldn't just let this go, considering all that was happening...

I did know beyond a shadow of a doubt that Michael had always had a thing for Julia, and would stoop to any level. Julia, on the other hand, I had more respect for, and knew that she would never do anything to jeopardize our friendship, nor hurt the girls and me. I would just have to weigh all the possibilities, however, I would give my best friend the benefit of the doubt. There was no way she would do that to me. Still, I had a nagging curiosity that evening, accompanied by an awful feeling in my gut.

Did I think that was Michael's affair? No, not really, because Julia lived in Texas. Did I think that it was possible that Michael and Julia had a one-night stand, and made a baby? Yes, I did believe it was possible, because when I thought about it, I remembered that Julia was in California for an extended visit, and about three to four weeks after returning to Texas, she announced her pregnancy.

The more I thought about it, the more I got angry, and began to wonder; I had to be reasonable before drawing any conclusions though. Firstly, Madison was born with Duarte Galactosemia, which was extremely rare, and only happened every one in forty thousand births, and it just so happened that my lifetime best friend's daughter, Katie, was also born with Duarte Galactosemia.

I was starting to think there was nothing coincidental about Katie resembling Millie, or the Duarte Galactosemia. This truly made me feel sick even thinking about it. I loved Julia as if she were my own sister, and did not want to believe that this could ever have happened.

She would never do anything so deleterious. There was no way I would even consider bringing this up with her, although I would discuss it with Michael.

Later that evening when Michael and I had some time to spend alone in our room, I told him that I had something I wanted to discuss with him. His face changed color, and he got extremely defensive with me. I told him I didn't want to argue, but just wanted to discuss a couple of things.

I told him that the conversation concerned Julia and her baby, Katie. He had this unpleasant look on his face and said, "What about them?"

I said, *"Michael, you and I both know that you have always had a thing for Julia. You also know that Julia became pregnant while she was here in California, and that her and Jonathan have not been intimate with each other in a long time."* He said, "So what?" I replied, *"So what? I find it a little peculiar that the baby resembles Millie, was born with the same genetic disorder as Madison, and I noticed your reaction when you saw her earlier! Tell me, Michael, that the two of you were not stupid enough to get together while she was here, and do something so fricken low!"*

Michael got so nervous that I wasn't sure what he was going to do or say. For a moment, I figured I would just get the usual remarks, which were, "You always think that I'm cheating on you!" *"Michael?"* I said. *"Would you mind telling me what's going on here?"*

47

"It wasn't all my fault, you can't just blame me!" At that moment, I don't think he realized the words he had just blurted out. My body and mind felt as if they had been anesthetized, and I wasn't sure what to think or do. This had become a fiery conversation, and he said, "You always want to blame me for everything!" I said, *"So, who should I blame, me?"*

I wasn't getting anywhere, and the conversation seemed to be going in circles. My nerves were already shot to hell, and it wasn't going to benefit me at all to worry about whether or not they had had an affair. I couldn't exactly change it if they had. I could honestly say that nothing Michael did surprised me anymore.

He seemed to be lacking in his ability to use common sense, and always found a way to justify whatever he did, and at the same time believed that it was the right thing to do. How could I confront Julia about it? Should I risk a lifelong friendship to do so? On the other hand, could I just let it rest?

We were still in the midst of summer, and Julia was heading back to Texas with her family. Jonathan had been having some problems with a compulsive disorder, and was suffering from manic depression. He was such a Southern gentlemen, but was starting to show sides of himself that none of us knew, and it was obviously putting a strain on their marriage. He seemed to be taking a colossal amount of antidepressant drugs, along with some extracurricular recreational ones as well.

Julia had called me many times crying her eyes out over many different situations. Since she lived in Texas, it was difficult to reach out, and give her a big hug over the phone. However, I would try to comfort her as best I could in her times of need.

Things had really started to heat up between the two of them. One afternoon she arrived home from work, only to be confronted by Jonathan holding a shotgun in the living room. He had been hiding it under the cushion of the sofa, loaded, with two children in the house! This was insane, and was not the Southern gentleman we had all grown to know and love.

When Julia cried out to him in fear, and asked what he was doing with the gun, he replied that he had bought it for his protection. Why did he suddenly need protection? It wasn't likely that Julia or his children were suddenly going to attack him.

Julia was terrified, and immediately called the police. I told her that considering his mental state was so unstable, it would be a good idea for her to be very careful around him. I thought that he might try to hurt her, or the children. He was no doubt angry, and I had a terrible feeling that I was going to get a phone call saying that he had killed her and the kids, possibly even himself.

The police finally showed up; the situation obviously warranting immediate attention by the authorities, and she had him arrested.

Julia soon filed for a legal separation, and Jonathan moved into his own place. He did not intend to grant her a divorce, and would fight her all the way. He kept showing up at the house in bouts of rage, and finally Julia was forced to file a restraining order, in the hopes that it would keep her and the kids safe.

Meanwhile she was terrified that he might break into the house, and kill her and the kids. If he couldn't have her, he didn't want anyone else to have her. As much as we loved him, I kept telling her to look over her shoulder. He obviously had become very unstable, and I didn't trust his intentions, especially after hiding a loaded shotgun in the house.

48

Michael and I had been having our own problems; our property manager had just informed us that the owner was selling the house we were living in, and had given us thirty days notice to find another place to live. It was always a nuisance to move, but this time it was not just a nuisance, we were going to miss the friends we had made.

We ran into lots of difficulties finding a place, because we wanted to buy, but didn't want to rush into anything, and we couldn't find an acceptable rental. Mom and Dad decided that we could move in with them temporarily, while we were looking for our own place. This seemed to be somewhat reasonable, with the exception of seven of us all being squished like sardines into a tiny two-bedroom apartment, with, I might add, our pets, Muffin and Oliver.

Michael was still up to no good, and we were constantly arguing. Well, that was whenever he decided that he had a family to come home to, as he was still coming home late from work every evening, exhausted, and with a multitude of excuses.

My dad would never dream that Michael would be doing anything he wasn't supposed to be doing. He thought Michael was as pure as the driven snow, and kept saying, "For craps sakes, leave the poor guy alone, he's busting his ass out there working for you, and when he comes home, he's tired!" What was wrong with everyone? Why was I the only one that knew Michael was up to no good?

Many nights Michael didn't come home until after eight o'clock, and he always smelt of alcohol, sweat, or both. Our girls were now starting to comment on Dad's appearance, and the fact that he reeked of alcohol. Obviously they were not sure what the odor was, but they knew Dad smelt bad.

After several evenings, I finally decided that I couldn't take any more of this crap and had to confront him. So I waited until I was home alone, and called him at work.

"Michael, I know that you are up to no good, and I know you are seeing someone else!" He completely denied everything, which didn't surprise me at all. After another fiery conversation I said, *"Michael, I do not like the manner in which you are coming home, and if this is the life you choose, then don't come home!"*

Just as if it were a tape recording, once again he said, "All I do is work my ass off and come straight home to my family, and I am tired of you always accusing me of being with someone else!" This argument would not be the last one, and our marriage was definitely on the rocks. His heavenly emerald green eyes that I used to get lost in were gone.

Now, when I looked into his eyes all I could see were lies and deception. I felt so strongly about his behavior that I decided to take off my wedding ring.

However, our problems seemed small in comparison with the news we then received. A good friend of ours, Nancy's sister, Janet, had lost her battle with cancer, and passed away. We would always remember her as a beautiful young woman, and she would forever be held dear to our hearts, especially the precious memories of the time she dressed up as an adorable, yet hysterical clown, for one of our girls' birthday parties, and brought such joy to all of the children.

After hearing this news, our problems were petty, compared to the loss of a life. Death seemed to somehow always put things into perspective.

Mom and Dad's property manager found out that we were living with them, and gave us two weeks to move out. We hadn't had any luck at all finding another suitable place to live within our girls' school district, and our time had run out. She gave my parents an ultimatum; either we moved out, or she was going to evict them.

So... Michael, the girls, and I were forced to move into a motel and now, you might say, we were homeless. I couldn't believe that, on top of everything else, we were now homeless, and

Michael still couldn't care less! This was heartbreaking. Was it ever going to end?

This was no first-class hotel, but your run-of-the-mill motel with two small beds, one shower, one toilet, a TV, and the most repulsive smell of smoke you could ever imagine. The view outside was that of the dark side of living, including the likes of prostitutes checking into the rooms across the parking lot from us, and to think, all this for just one hundred dollars per night!

All five of us, with our pets, crammed into this tiny little room. We had no fridge, so every meal; breakfast, lunch, and dinner, was restaurant or fast food. All of us were miserable living there, with the exception of Michael. I just didn't understand him at all; it didn't even faze him. I personally did not want my girls living like that. We had to find a house.

Every morning Michael would leave for work, and I would drop the girls off at school. Mom and I searched the newspapers, and drove around in the hope of finding some type of rental for us. This went on for about a week, and had become very depressing.

Still nothing seemed to faze Michael, and I thought if it were up to him, he would have lived in a motel forever. Finally, we got a break, when Mom happened to be driving around in a somewhat nice area, and found us a rental. It wasn't exactly a beautiful place, but it was certainly better than living in a motel, and would just have to do for a while. It was a two-bedroom apartment, with one-and-a-half bathrooms, and a combination kitchen and family room. A palace compared to the motel.

Our girls had been through so much already, and I would have done anything to make them feel comfortable with their lives. Part of that was making sure that they had a bedroom to sleep in. Michael and I had agreed to let the girls share the two bedrooms, which were ten by ten in size. Millie had one of them, and Madeline and Madison shared the other one. Most of our belongings were in storage. Michael and I slept on a rollout mattress on the family room floor.

The lust or passion I once felt for Michael was now hindered by hurt, anger, and a strong conviction that he belonged to someone else. How do you make love to your husband when you feel as if another woman is in bed with the two of you, and it isn't really you he is making love to?

It was no longer lovemaking for him, but more a sexual fantasy. I just felt like a warm body for him to use, and with every breath, every movement, I knew that he was not really there with me. Where were those feverish, intense feelings we once shared?

Why was he still telling me that he loved me? There didn't seem to be any emotion behind those words. The passion in his lips had gone cold, and I felt as if I were kissing a stranger. As the two of us lay there, embraced in what seemed to be emptiness, my heart broke, and my mind wondered what had happened to that fiery sexual desire the two of us had once shared.

All those vehement and impassioned moments we had shared throughout the years had become foreign. I told Michael that I could no longer do it; it was not lovemaking, but his unbridled sexual desire to fill some compulsive sexual fantasy he had, which was obviously not directed at me.

Michael's response was, "You know that I have only been with you, and that I love only you! I'm tired of you always thinking that I'm with someone else! So why don't you want to be with me?" I said, *"You know why, Michael. I can't be with you when I know in my heart that you are with someone else. I cannot be here for you to play out your sexual fantasies."*

49

By this time, I was doing part time debt collecting for a friend at a marble fabricating company. The phone usually rang non-stop, and that day was no exception. Around mid-morning, I received a phone call from Julia's sister, Jennifer.

Just hearing her voice sent a chill up and down my spine; I knew there had to be something wrong, because she had never called me at work before. As I sat, trembling in my chair, Jennifer told me she had bad news. At that moment, my fears of something happening to Julia had become real. However, she wasn't calling with regard to Julia, but Jonathan; he had committed suicide, inside Julia's home, which was heartbreaking.

She said that Julia and the two children were fine physically, and that he hadn't harmed them. Jonathan had gone over to Julia's house pleading for her to take him back. Since she had a restraining order, and feared for her life, she politely asked him to leave, or she would have to call the police.

At that point, he broke into the house with a gun. He had already cut the phone lines, and threw Julia onto the floor, where he held her at gunpoint. Her son had run out of the house to get help, and use the neighbors' phone to call the police. Katie, the baby, was in her room taking a nap, and was really too young to understand what was going on anyway.

Apparently, when Jonathan had her down on the floor at gunpoint, with the lights out, the SWAT team showed up. When this happened he was startled, and Julia was able to get away from him, and run down the hall into the baby's room.

He followed her down the hall and by then, the SWAT team was pulling Julia and the baby out the window to safety. As if saying goodbye, he looked at them with deep-seated sorrow in his eyes, turned, and headed back down the hallway toward the kitchen.

It had been a very gloomy evening to begin with; the winds were howling, and rain was pouring down by the buckets, thunder rumbled, and lightning lit up the evening sky. Not a sound could be heard from Jonathan inside Julia's house.

She and the kids were safe inside a neighbor's house with the paramedics, and it would be hours before the SWAT team would finally gain entry into the home, only to find Jonathan's lifeless body lying in a pool of blood, with a single bullet wound to his head.

It was very tragic. I guessed our Southern gentleman really had endured a lot of pain and anguish, and decided that he didn't want to live without Julia anymore. I was so sorry that he had taken his own life, but I was also so thankful that he did not take Julia and the kids' lives as well. He was at peace now, and we would always hold memories of him close to our hearts.

The holidays were here once again. They were such a special time of year for us, and I tried to ignore our marital problems around our girls, and avoid any arguing. However, that year the intensity and anger that had built up between Michael and myself over his cheating, which he still denied, was making all of us miserable. Madeline and Madison still thought that Dad was Mr. Wonderful, but Millie and I were both on the same page, so to speak, and both had a strong feeling that he was cheating on me, on us.

Michael's company party was coming up, and he wanted me to go with him, but I told him I wouldn't even consider it. He wanted us to pretend, and show off to all his coworkers how happily married we were! He knew that I wouldn't go with him to the party, but he brought the tickets home anyway. I was livid and said, *"I told you that I wasn't going to go with you and pretend!"* He said, "I was hoping that you would have changed your mind, and gone with me!" Michael knew all along that I wasn't going to go with him; it was all part of his game plan. He didn't bring the tickets home for him and I, as one would expect. Yeah, right, he was so broken up about me not wanting to go with him. The tickets were obviously for him, and whomever he was doodling.

On the day of the Christmas party, he was like a cat on a hot tin roof! Why? He knew that I wasn't going with him to the party, but I did tell him that he was welcome to go alone if he liked. The party just happened to be at a fancy hotel, and the guests were to be accommodated there overnight.

So... I figured he would be sleeping with the person that he said didn't exist. I said, *"Michael, go to your party and enjoy yourself, I hope she is worth it! However, if you go to the party, I will know that you are not going to be by yourself, or sleeping by yourself, and then you and I will have more problems."* He said, "I told you the ticket is for you, and there is no one else!"

Michael, it seemed, watched the clock constantly throughout that day, just as if he were missing the meeting of a lifetime. He was so fidgety, more than I had ever seen. The party time came and went, and I could just see the disappointment in his face. I guessed he must have stood someone up. Oh, the poor thing, waiting for Mr. Wonderful to arrive, and take her to the Christmas party! Did she even know he was married? Of course, this was all just speculation; according to Michael, there was no one else, he was a saint, and I was just imagining all of this. I said, *"Michael, why don't you just admit it? The truth shall set you free!"* He just looked at me with a fiery look in his eyes, as if I were some kind of a nut.

50

Christmas Day had arrived, and typically our house was full of joy and happiness, but there wasn't going to be any that year. The girls could tell that Mommy and Dad were having major problems in their marriage and maybe, just maybe, they were starting to see that Mommy was not nuts, and that Daddy was up to no good. The girls did not deserve to have their holidays ruined like that.

I had told Michael that I absolutely positively did not want him to buy me any gifts, and that if he did, I would not accept them. I didn't buy him anything, but I did get him gifts from the girls. After all he was their father.

When we opened our gifts and Michael saw that I hadn't bought him anything, he was devastated. Oh, such tears we had! He, on the other hand, paid no attention to what I had said about not wanting any gifts from him, and bought them anyway, which caused quite a commotion. To me, they were all just guilt gifts. He always bought me guilt gifts; every time I had ever been suspicious of his actions, it was almost guaranteed that he would come home with a bouquet of flowers or a rose that day.

After the girls were finished, and excited about all their gifts from Santa, Michael had to once again, make a big scene in front of them, and make me look like the jerk. He leaned forward and asked me to give him a Christmas kiss. I said, *"No! I'm not kissing you!"* He said, "Why not?" And I said, *"Because I don't want to!"* He said, "Oh, come on, give me a kiss."

He found it very amusing, and was chuckling. I said, *"No! Why should I kiss you when you already have someone else to kiss?"* Madeline and Madison said, "Come on, Mommy, give Daddy a kiss!" But I said, *"No, your father doesn't deserve a kiss."* I was furious that he had put me on the spot like that to try and score points with our daughters.

I said, *"Michael, the only thing I want from you for Christmas is for you to be honest for once, and admit to me and to yourself that you are in fact having an affair. Therefore, I will not give you a kiss."*

Millie, Madeline, and Madison had gone into their rooms to put away some of their Christmas gifts and play with others. While they were all in their rooms, my plan was to have a serious discussion with Michael about his behavior.

So, with fire in my eyes, and my heart beating wildly, I said, *"Michael, you know what? You have a lot of balls making a "kiss me" scene in front of our girls! You make me want to throw up, trying to make them think that all the arguing is my fault; making them think that you love me so much, and I won't even give you a kiss! Oh, yes, poor Daddy! Michael, let me tell you something, buddy. You have until the end of this month, which is December 31st, to come clean with this affair. I know that you are screwing around, and it's time you admitted it! I am not going into another new year of you doing this to the girls and me. You'd better come clean, or I will divorce your fricken ass!"*

For the first time ever, Michael didn't say a word; his mood was completely somber, his face beet red, and without expression.

When my parents came over to visit us that afternoon, they were puzzled by how quiet and distant Michael was. He was never distant with them, and always quite friendly, but not that day. He had things on his mind; things that I believed were going to change his life.

A couple days later, I met with a good family friend of ours, Jack. I always confided in him, he was my true friend. He said, "It is highly unlikely, and there is no way that Michael is ever going to admit to having an affair! He will never confess." I disagreed with him, and I said, *"I truly believe that Michael is having an affair, and I won't give up until he tells the truth. I cannot and will not allow our marriage to go on like this."*

Jack thought perhaps Michael could benefit from joining the Men's Christian Group that he belonged to, but Michael had never had any interest in joining.

The New Year was approaching rapidly, and Michael still hadn't confessed to having done anything wrong. I was still hoping that he would come to his senses, and admit it. Deep down, I just knew that he was cheating on me, and it was making me crazy! On December 30th, he went to work as if he had had nothing at all on his mind that morning. Millie, Madeline, Madison, and I went shopping to get some New Year's eve goodies.

We had a great day, and bought tons of goodies. The girls and I were thinking about going to see a movie that evening, but first we wanted to relax for a while.

Since we had been gone most of the day, I thought it might be a good idea to check our voicemail messages before we went out again. The last message on the voicemail was from Michael. I didn't think anything of it really. It sounded like his typical daily phone call. He said, "Hi, Hon, I think that you and I need to sit down and have a talk."

51

"You were right, I have gone astray, and have been cheating on you and the girls. I want to make a fresh start; I just can't go on like this, and I think we should sit down and talk about it."

I couldn't believe how calm his voice was on the answering machine. It sounded more like he was buying a loaf of bread! He didn't even have the balls to tell me in person, he had to hide behind voicemail, and even then, there was absolutely no emotion in his voice whatsoever.

Even though my gut feeling all along had been that he was cheating, to actually hear it on the voicemail was an intense emotional blow. I started shaking, and couldn't believe what I was hearing. I played the message back a couple of times in disbelief, and then saved it.

The girls were in their bedrooms, and had no idea what was going on. I didn't want to say anything to them yet. Oh, my God, I wanted to throw up. What was I going to do? My heart was racing and I wasn't sure if I was going to throw up, have diarrhea, pass out, or a combination of all three. I managed to make it down the hall and into the bathroom.

I felt as if my entire body was going to shake loose, and become detached from reality. I sat down and at that moment, Millie walked in and saw that Mommy was trembling and that obviously something was wrong. "Mommy, what's the matter?" she asked.

I was trying desperately to take deep breaths, and calm myself down. I asked her to please bring me a glass of water and with that, I proceeded to tell her that our suspicions about Michael had been right. I told her that he had left me a voicemail confirming what we already knew...

Millie and I hugged as we both tried to compose ourselves. Right then, I hated his guts, and all the lies that went with him. Millie was beyond angry, and felt the same as I did. Madeline and Madison were still in their rooms. I would tell them, but not yet.... I needed to talk to Michael first, and see where we were going to go from there.

Since Michael was on his way home from work, Millie and I decided that Madeline and Madison should go over to Grandma and Grandpa's house for a slumber party. So we picked up some videos and goodies for them, and dropped them off over there for the evening. Millie would stay home with me just in case anything should happen.

However, she would stay in her room while Michael and I talked. I promised her I would try not to go ballistic because I knew that stress was not good for the life-threatening diseases I had already endured; it played havoc with my system, and sent it into a flare state, which was in fact life threatening.

By the time Millie and I returned home from dropping off Madeline and Madison, Michael was home from work, and already in the shower. My inner self was trying desperately to calm down. I kept telling myself to calm down, take deep breaths, and that it was going to be alright, when deep down I knew that it really wasn't going to be alright. It seemed like he was in the shower for an eternity. Millie and I were sitting on the sofa, hugging each other, in an attempt to find some comfort in this nightmare.

Michael walked down the hall, just as if the birds were chirping and flowers blooming on a bright, spring day. But this was no bright, spring day; it was a gloomy winter's day, and the skies were wreaking havoc over our family room. I couldn't believe that he actually had the nerve to walk into the family room and say "Hi, Hon!"

I truly thought he was missing some brain cells! He walked over, stared at me, and said, "Why is Millie here? I thought you and I were going to have a talk?" I said, *"We are going to have a talk. Millie knows all about this, and has for a long time."* Michael's facial expression turned bleak, and somewhat wrathful.

Millie went into her room, and Michael and I sat on separate sofas across from each other in the family room. I said, *"Michael, I cannot believe that you have the nerve to leave such a disgusting voicemail telling me that you have been cheating! Don't you have any shame? You want to talk, fine, let's talk!"*

So with absolutely no expression or emotion in his face, Michael started to tell me what I already knew. I sat quietly in disbelief, still not sure that I was really hearing this, or if it was a nightmare. The feelings I had were incomprehensible, and just cannot be put into words.

He said, "I know that I did wrong, and I just can't live with myself anymore. It's just becoming too much for me to carry around, and I know that you have known for a long time, and I finally just decided to confess to you."

I said, *"And?"* He said, "And, I'm begging you to please forgive me, and give me another chance! I want us to start over, and be a family again." The room had become dead silent; I wasn't really sure how to approach this without having a stroke, and losing complete control of what little sanity I had left.

Now it was my turn, and one could only imagine what I wanted to say. *"So, Michael, all the times I confronted you about cheating, or having an affair you lied straight to my face? You even spat in my face, and now you want to start over?"* He said, "You know that I love you and the girls!"

I said, *"You are nothing but a bastard! You have done nothing but lie to me for almost twenty years, and now you are asking me to forgive you? Are you insane? All the times you came home late from work with those preposterous excuses, having our girls think that I was crazy, and that all you were doing was making a living, you were with another woman?* He said, "Yes, and I'm sorry for that."

I said, *"I want to know who this woman is, and how long this has been going on?"* Michael proceeded to tell me it had been going on for a couple of months, and I said, *"Get real, Michael, we both know that you have been screwing around for years! You are sitting here asking for my forgiveness, and you can't even tell me the truth? You are nothing but a son-of-a-bitch, and you'll never change! I should have known from the very beginning. Now I'm going to ask you one more time, how long has this been going on?"* Well, his response went from a couple of months, to a couple of years, and finally to ten plus years. I came completely unglued. I said, *"You were cheating on me while I was being treated for cancer?"* What followed was even more shocking than the confession of his affair.

Michael said, "What do you mean you had cancer?" I said, *"What? You didn't know I had cancer. Oh, my God, there has to be something wrong with you for you to forget that your wife had cancer! You don't remember the surgeries to remove the malignant tumor, or being treated at the medical center?"* He said, "Well, I remember you being sick, and having something wrong with your neck, but I didn't know it was cancer."

By this time, I was boiling over, and he was still sitting there without any display of emotion whatsoever. He was obviously so wrapped up in his affair that he never even acknowledged me being so sick! There was definitely something wrong with that picture.

After discussing his affair in detail, I guess he decided that he looked like a real asshole in forgetting how sick I had been, and said, "I'm sorry that I forgot you had cancer, it just slipped my mind." I said, *"I disagree with you, simply because when something so major takes place, especially with someone you love, like your wife, you don't forget the traumatic moments like when they are diagnosed with cancer! Michael, if this means that while I underwent open-heart surgery to remove that tumor from behind my heart, and was in coronary intensive care at Stanford, you were out doodling your girlfriend, then I feel sorry for you, Michael, you need help."* His reply was, "What do you mean? You think I'm a couch case?" I simply said, *"Michael, you need help."*

Well, the conversation had come this far, but I still wanted to know with whom he had been having the affair. So I said, *"Okay, hot shot, I want to know who it is you've been screwing?"* Without any hesitation, he sat his coffee cup down and said, "Martha." I said, *"Martha who?"*

He said, "Martha Williams." And I said, *"The African-American lady from work?"* Once again my body was starting to feel wobbly. He said, "No!" And then he looked me straight in the eyes, and said, "Martha Williams, Julia's mother!"

The words that came out of his mouth couldn't have been real; I thought that I was going to throw up. I couldn't move or speak. I screamed, *"Michael, this has to be the most disgusting thing that I have ever heard! You have been having an affair with my best friend's mother? This has to be a sick joke! Is there something wrong with you? Michael, you are the fucking scum of the earth!*

You obviously will stoop to any level to get what you want, won't you? How could you do this to me? She is old enough to be your mother! Maybe you do need a couch, and you definitely need psychiatric help. I just can't fricken believe that you would stoop so low as to have an affair with my best friend's mother! Why, I want to know, why her? You had such a thing for Julia that you had to fantasize about her mother? She is a fricken shriveled up old woman, and this is repulsive! Do you love her?" He said, "No, I don't love her, but I do care about her, and wouldn't want anything to happen to her."

By then, I think I had froth coming out of my mouth, and steam bellowing from my entire body; I felt like I was on fire. All Michael kept saying was that he was sorry, and that it had nothing to do with me. It was just a bad choice that he had made. I considered myself to be a good wife and mother.

I said, *"Michael, she was either really good, or you were really bad! I just cannot fricken believe this. Do you realize how many lives you have affected by doing this? You have ruined our lives, and obviously messed up the lifetime loyal friendship that Julia and I shared."*

If that didn't give me a heart attack, nothing would. All through the years when Michael was supposed to be out looking for work, at the union, or unemployment office, he was over at Martha's house servicing her, and I don't mean her washing machine.

Now, when I think back to some of the coincidental things that had happened throughout the years, it all started to make sense. Like the time we went to Great America. I couldn't put my finger on it then, but I knew something was wrong when we met Julia with her family, which included Martha. In our little circle, the air was quite thick, and I smelled a rat. Unfortunately, I just couldn't figure out why. But, now I knew why; they had been sleeping together!

I said, *"No, Michael, I will not forgive you! You have lied to me for many years now, and I cannot forgive you for doing something so hurtful and repulsive."* Michael said, "But I told you the truth, and you said if I told you the truth that we could start over! What good did it do for me to confess to you? I would have been better off not telling you!" I said, *"Well, Michael, that was your choice. It is one thing to have an affair, but it is another thing to have one with someone that is almost like a relative to me!"* He said, "I said I was sorry, and that should be the end of it!" I said, *"I don't know what I am going to do at this point, but I do know that you'd better get a vasectomy, because I don't need any more surprises, and I want you to go to a counselor."*

He said, "A marriage counselor?" I said, *"No! I didn't do this, you are perverted, and this is totally sick. She is thirty-three years older than you, and my best friend's mother! I also want you to go to church and pray. And if I were you, I would get down on my hands and knees and beg for forgiveness. Don't you ever call me your 'Hon' again, and whatever you do, don't ever say you love me! Those are just empty words now."*

52

The next afternoon was quite stressful for us; Michael had come home from work and had several things that needed to be taken care of including calling Martha to tell her that I knew about the affair. He also had to call Julia to tell her that my suspicions about him having an affair had been right all along, and that the affair was with her mother.

Madeline and Madison were home by then, and the two of them, along with Millie and I, had a long discussion about their father's behavior. Millie knew who the woman was, but I felt Madeline and Madison were too young, and it wasn't necessary for them to know.

Michael called Martha and the funny thing was, he always had trouble remembering phone numbers, but not hers; he dialed it without a problem. It was almost as if he were numb to what was going on around him. His phone call was so subtle; it was almost like inviting someone out for a cup of coffee.

He said, "Hi Martha, it's Michael. Listen, I have some bad news for you; Sara knows about our affair." Unfortunately, I could only hear what HE was saying. He said, "I'm sorry, I had to tell her, she knew anyway."

Without saying a word, I grabbed the phone from him, so that I could hear firsthand what she was saying. She didn't know that I had the phone and said, "Why did you tell her? Why didn't you lie to her?" That was enough for me, and I handed the phone back to Michael, and had to walk over and sit down on the sofa.

Michael told me that she wanted to speak to me, and I started to scream. She had the audacity to want to speak to me after ruining all of our lives! She was nothing but a fucking bitch and a slut, and I didn't ever want to speak to her again! All through his entire conversation with her, he still showed no emotion. I thought a corpse would have had more life in it than he did.

Later on that afternoon, Michael called Julia to break the news to her. Poor Julia had just lost her husband a month earlier, and her frame of mind was far from stable. Once again, Michael called and said, "Hi, Julia, how are you?" Then he said, "Hey, you know how Sara has been telling you that she thought I was having an affair? Well, she was right; I have been having an affair, and it's with your mother."

I was standing there listening, and it made me sick to my stomach; it was almost as if he were getting pleasure out of telling her. I could hear her screaming and cursing at him on the other end of the phone, and he said, "I'm sorry, and I hope this doesn't interfere with your friendship."

Julia and I, both in tears, spoke to each other after he was finished. It was incomprehensible to both of us, and we thought they were both perverted and in need of psychiatric help.

This situation had put a lot of stress on my system, and consequently my medications had to be increased. By then I was taking over five hundred pills per month to control my life-threatening illnesses.

My doctors kept telling me to avoid stressful situations, but that was easier said than done, especially when married to someone that lacked common sense, and had no concept of consequences until it was too late. When I thought of all the times Michael would try to convince me that he was not with anyone other than me, I got sick to my stomach.

Michael carried on like he didn't have a care in the world, and as if none of this had ever happened, and he wanted me to do the same; just sweep it under the rug, and forget it had ever happened. How could he expect me to do that? I didn't think the man had a conscience. How could I forget about it? I had decided that our wedding rings no longer held any meaning, and had just become another piece of jewelry. So I sold them. Why should I have kept them? It would have been a big lie to wear them, and pretend that we were happily married. Michael didn't understand why I sold the rings, and was very unhappy about it, but that's life.

SARA TENACI
THAT'S ANOTHER CUP OF COFFEE

53

After all I had been through with Michael, there really wasn't too much trust in our house regarding men. Millie had been dating Eric, a young man from her school, but although they were crazy about each other, there was something about the relationship that made me uncomfortable. He had many good qualities, but he lacked respect for my daughter, which I thought was essential.

It had been a very limited relationship, based on Millie's morals and values, which eventually led to him wanting his space, and to date other girls. This devastated Millie, and she cried for days, which was heartbreaking for me to see her go through. Eventually though, she moved on with her life, and was able to see that, even though she had cared deeply for him, she had not been in love with him.

Throughout all the heartache, I could honestly say that the one thing, or should I say the three things, that kept me sane were my three beautiful daughters. I could never have gotten through any of this without them. No matter how dismal things got, I could always count on them to raise my spirits, as well as their own.

Humor is a good medicine, and that particular week was no exception. Millie and I were going to the Laundromat, but noticed that we had no detergent. So, one would think it would be easier just to go and buy another box, but being rushed for time, I decided to use something else. We got to the Laundromat, and Millie and I placed our clothes into the jumbo machines.

I poured the powder into the machines, and Millie said, "Mommy, don't tell me that you are using dishwasher soap? Don't even tell me, I don't want to know!" I said, *"Yes, it's true, our clothes are going to be dishwasher clean!"*

The two of us laughed hysterically, and I think the other patrons must have thought we had lost our marbles, but hey, laughter is the best medicine, and the clothes turned out fresh and clean.

Speaking of dishwasher detergent, Madeline had decided one evening that she was going to fill the dishwasher for me. She seemed to be doing just fine, and I didn't think a whole lot could go wrong with filling a dishwasher.

After she was finished, she turned it on, and went into her room to play. I happened to be sitting in the family room when suddenly, out of the corner of my eye, I could see colossal, fluffy bubbles pouring out of the dishwasher, and all over the kitchen. We had a very tiny kitchen, and it quickly became covered with bubbles, which resembled fluffy clouds. I found it pretty amusing, but Madeline didn't think it was too funny, and thought she was going to get into trouble.

Apparently, she had used the liquid dish soap, instead of the dishwasher powder, which caused our kitchen to take on a heavenly atmosphere. We all certainly had another good laugh that day.

A couple of days later the girls were all playing a game together, and Madison was trying to point out to her sisters that they must play fairly, and cheating was not allowed. I had always told the girls that "cheaters never prosper," and Madison, even though young remembered this.

So there they were playing monopoly, and Madison said, "Don't you know that cheaters never prostitute?" We all came completely unglued, and filled with laughter. It's times like those that help you forget all of your problems, even if for just a moment; they are wonderful memories, and well worth every moment.

I had decided to set some goals for myself, one of which included getting my Real Estate license. It had been several years since I was in school, so it would definitely pose a challenge for me. I also wanted to write a book; every morning I made a pit stop at my favorite coffee shop, which gave me some quiet quality time to reflect on my life, and capture it on paper. The people in there were, for the most part, patient, but it often looked like a line of people waiting at the Pearly Gates of Heaven for their orders. Periodically I met with some friends there, and we would sit and talk about our everyday lives.

Within the space of a month, Millie baptized my niece, Cristina; Madison and my other niece, Livia, made their First Holy Communion; and Millie made her Confirmation, and asked my sister-in-law, Maria, to sponsor her. All of these ceremonies were beautiful, but Michael didn't attend any of them because of the obvious marital problems that were still lurking in the shadows.

Months had come and gone since Michael confessed to his infidelity, and he still brought me flowers and cards. The card that really got to me was the one that said, "Please be a little more patient with me."

I said, *"Michael, you want me to be patient with you? I have been patient almost half of my life regarding your infidelity, and yet you still want more? I don't have another twenty years in me to be patient with you! You are a grown up now, not a young child learning right from wrong, and asking Mommy or Daddy for another chance. I am not your mother, and in case you hadn't noticed or perhaps you forgot, I am supposed to be your wife. You also have three children here that you are supposed to be setting examples for!"*

Before I could go for my State Real Estate exam, I had to take and pass the final exam. For the final, you could write the exam in any business office of your choosing with a proctor. I chose our good friend, Jack's, office. Millie and I both went to his office, and while I racked my brain with the test, the two of them had a good time playing in the other room.

Even though Jack was a big kid, he was a very strong Christian with an infinite amount of faith. Millie and Jack were like two peas in a pod, and she really looked up to him. Jack and his wife, Joanne, also had a daughter, Jackie, who had just gotten married to a fine Italian gentleman named Nino.

After I finished my test, Jack graded it, and faxed it in for the official results. Fortunately for me, I got an A, and I was extremely satisfied with these results. The business school would mail me my certification.

Before we left, and to break the ice, he decided to do some gymnastics in the main lobby of his office. Millie and I were hysterical, and we gave him a nine point nine; giving him a perfect ten would have made us appear biased. I had never walked away from a conversation with Jack without feeling good about it, and knowing that we were truly blessed to have him in our lives.

Once again, the holiday season had arrived, and Millie had been coming home every day talking about a young man at school named Bryce; she said he had the most "beautiful blue eyes." I didn't want to say too much; I figured it would be better to just listen for a while, and see just where this new friendship was going to go. However, I did have a feeling that she was starting to like this young man, and she seemed pretty happy about their friendship.

She would come home, and tell me how he literally picked her up, and carried her on his shoulders to one of her classes, as if she were a little toy. Well, actually she was pretty petite at less than five feet two inches, one hundred five pounds, compared to him at six feet.

Their friendship seemed to be growing, and she was very happy; I hadn't seen her this happy in a long time. By the first week of December, they were exchanging e-mails, and seemed to have quite a bit in common. I am not sure how I got a chance to speak with him online, but I did, and he seemed to be a very wholesome young man. One evening, while Millie was speaking with him online, she was taken by surprise when he asked her out; she was really fidgety, beyond anything I had ever seen before with her.

When he arrived at our house, Millie wanted me to open the door, and I was more than happy to meet this young man, and see exactly whom my daughter seemed to be falling for. I opened the door, and there stood a nice looking, bright-eyed young man, with a smile that lit up the room. We introduced ourselves and shook hands, but once he saw Millie it no longer mattered whether or not anyone else was in the room. It was obvious whom he had come to see.

Their first date was December 11th, and he took her to Santa Cruz Beach Boardwalk, and to play miniature golf. They had a wonderful time together. Millie and I talked afterwards, and I could tell that she could really fall for this guy.

Considering how she had gotten hurt with the last young man she dated, she wanted to take this new friendship slowly. Within a couple of weeks, they had become very close, and by mid-December he invited her to the Christmas Ball. She was ecstatic, and just couldn't believe it. Grandma had promised Millie that she would buy her first formal ball gown. So off to the mall we went, and Millie picked a really elegant black, silky mid-length party dress, covered in sparkles, and matching ankle strap black high heels. She was going to look beautiful.

On the evening of the dance, Grandma came over to do Millie's hair since she had expertise in that area. Madeline, Madison, and two of my nieces, Felicia and Livia, sat right next to her watching every single detail of Millie's preparation for the evening. It was a priceless moment, like something out of a fairytale. I was so happy for her, and just knew that night was going to be something special.

Grandma put the final touches on her hair, and she looked like a beautiful princess. When her night in shining armor showed up at our door, he looked very handsome in his coal black tuxedo with tails, complete with his beautiful smile.

Once again, when they saw each other and made eye contact, it was priceless and you could have heard a pin drop. With their faces glowing, they were finally off to have a magnificent evening at the Christmas Ball.

The evening had come to an end, and Millie and Bryce had the time of their lives at the ball, sealing it with a romantic kiss on our balcony. Millie walked in carrying a bunch of beautiful roses, and I just assumed she had gotten them at the Ball.

It seemed like the perfect romantic evening for a young couple and they looked so content in each other's arms. The suspense was killing me, and I just had to ask my daughter how her evening was; she was glowing, and I was so happy for her.

It appeared that she wanted me to start asking her questions first, so I did, *"Millie, I already know you had a wonderful evening, but where did these beautiful roses come from?"* Millie was overjoyed, and almost in tears when she started to explain the significance of the roses to me.

Apparently, after the Ball, and once back inside the Cadillac, Bryce reached back behind the seat, and grabbed the beautiful long-stemmed white rose with a fern, and said, "This is a sign of our friendship." By that time, she was already on the verge of tears, and then he reached back and picked up another rose, only this time it was a beautiful single long-stemmed red rose with a fern, and he said, "And this is a sign of our undying love in the future."

Oh my goodness, was that romantic or what? *"My goodness, Millie, this young man really is charming, isn't he?"* Millie said that when he gave her the white rose, she had almost lost it, and then when he gave her the red rose, she was overcome with joy. That evening was like a fairytale for Millie and Bryce, and my sense was that we were going to be seeing a lot of him.

Millie and Bryce had become quite an adorable couple; she met his family and they just adored her. Even though the two of them were becoming very close, and had so much in common, they still respectfully held on to their morals. I could tell that Millie was falling in love with him, and it appeared that he was falling in love with her too. But that wasn't for me to decide, and in talking with Millie, I just kept telling her to let their friendship and relationship blossom slowly.

They were unbelievably happy together. It was scary, and I knew that Millie was afraid that it was too good to be true. I just couldn't stand to see her heartbroken again, and I prayed for her happiness.

Michael and Bryce had never really gotten to know each other, and there was a distinct wall between them. Madeline and Madison were just crazy about him. Actually, I thought that Madison had a crush on him, which was too cute. He was really good with the kids, and seemed to fit in quite well with our little family.

Christmas shopping season was in full bloom, and Bryce and his family had picked Millie up several times to take her shopping with them, and out to eat. I thought she had adopted them as her second family, and she thought they were wonderful. It seemed like a dream to see two young people so much in love, having so much fun together.

Millie, Madeline, Madison, and I went out for a nice Christmas Eve dinner, and afterwards Millie joined Bryce and his family at their house. They had a wonderful time. This was not just the traditional Christmas Eve, but also a lovely evening on which Bryce would officially ask Millie to be his steady girlfriend. So, on the 24th day of December 1999, Bryce and Millie became a couple.

That evening, Millie and I were up until about two a.m. filling all the stockings and putting out presents from Santa. I would fill her stocking and put out her gifts from Santa after she went to bed. In a few hours, the sun would rise, and it would turn out to be a beautiful Christmas morning.

The girls were all very happy with what Santa had brought them that year. We stayed home most of the day, and then headed over to my brother and sister-in-law's for Christmas dinner later in the day. Bryce was one of our guests, and as usual, Tony and Maria made this holiday another special and memorable day for all of us.

It was already New Year's Eve, and hard to believe that the year 2000 had arrived. Bryce was in Hawaii with his family, and had been calling Millie several times a day. She missed him something fierce. Our days were all pretty entertaining with my girls.

Michael and I still had a pretty platonic, or I should say nonexistent, relationship. I wasn't sure if we would ever be able to get back to being husband and wife again after what had happened to our marriage.

The New Year would probably zoom by just like the rest, and hopefully it would be a healthy, happy, and prosperous one for all of us. I had just had an MRI as a routine follow-up for the cancer, and it was always frightening waiting for test or lab results.

Pat, the nurse at my doctor's office, and I had actually become good friends over the past few years. As a matter of fact, I joined her and her family with their traditional Christmas Boutique. They always made such beautiful handmade crafts. I had been doing personalized cartoon prints on the computer, and I made them to order at their boutique. We all had so much fun together.

Within a couple of days of the MRI, I received a call from Pat. I was usually happy to hear from her but not that day. It wasn't exactly a "let's get together for lunch" call.

I could hear the anxiety in her voice, and having had cancer already, it was forever in the back of my mind that it was going to become active again. She said, "Not to alarm you, but there are changes in your MRI which need to be followed up."

Some time had passed since the fairytale began with Millie and Bryce. As a matter of fact on their one-month anniversary, Bryce told Millie that he loved her, and likewise from Millie. The relationship had always seemed too good to be true.

Bryce was moving away to college, and after careful consideration felt that a long distance relationship would not work, and therefore had broken up with Millie. She was crushed by this, and I didn't think I had ever seen her cry like that; it was devastating and heartbreaking to see her hurting so much. It certainly didn't make it any better breaking up so soon before Valentine's Day either. So now, as only one who has had their heart broken could imagine, Millie would have trouble trusting any young man's intentions, especially if he said he loved her with all sincerity.

54

The doctors were sending me for numerous diagnostic tests, some of which were positive and some negative. My body had never been typical textbook when it came to diagnosis; I remembered back when eleven doctors didn't know what was wrong with me, and I certainly hoped that didn't happen again. There was quite a difference this time though; I did have a great deal of confidence in my doctor's expertise.

Time just flies by when you are having fun, and it was already April of 2000, and I wondered who was going to be the fool? I was starting to have that little nagging feeling in my tummy, and thought perhaps I should call Michael's bluff with regards lying to me about being with anyone, that anyone being Martha.

So, I said, *"Michael, I'm just curious, when was the last time you were in contact with Martha?"* He said, "You know that I have not spoken to her since that day in 1998 when I called her to say it was over. Why would I want to call her? I have no reason to call her." I said, *"Michael, are you sure?"* And he said, "Yes, I'm sure!" So I said, *"I guess you won't mind if I call her then, will you?"* He said, "No, go right ahead!"

I hadn't spoken to her up until then, and my adrenaline was pumping out of control, but regardless of that I knew I had to do it. I couldn't hold onto it forever, so one day while Michael was at work I called her. I knew her number quite well, considering that I had grown up with her family.

My body was trembling, but I took a couple of deep breaths and called. She answered the phone in her very distinct Canadian accent, which was enough to get the fireball in my tummy burning. The anger and resentment I had felt toward her for so long poured out of my mouth in a heated froth.

"Is this the town slut?" I said. I knew that she recognized my voice immediately, and she began to laugh. I thought to myself what an idiot she was, and then I repeated, *"Are you the town slut?"* This time she replied with, "Yes, I am!"

I couldn't believe it, and she said, "Sara, is that you?" I said, *"Yes, it's me! It's time to get some answers as to what you have been doing all these years having an affair with my husband!"* She said, "What took you so long to call?" I said, *"I wasn't ready to call, but now I need some closure."*

At first, she denied the affair in its entirety. Our conversation became very heated, and she hung up the phone. My Italian blood was now boiling out of ever fiber of my being. I called her back and said, *"Don't you dare hang up on me! I am warning you, if you hang up I will make sure that all of your grandchildren know what kind of disrespectful slut you really are!"* Then she finally took me seriously, and decided she had better be reasonable and cooperate with what I needed to know.

I said, *"I want to know what happened and why? You were supposed to be my loyal friend. You took me on my very first Disneyland trip as a young girl, you love my girls and my family to pieces, why my husband? Do you not have any shame?"*

She said, "It was all Michael's fault, and I didn't want anything to do with him!" I said, *"If you didn't want anything to do with him, why were you playing out your sexual fantasies with him for over ten years? Do you have no conscience? Hello, do you remember your daughter and I being best friends? You know what? You two deserve each other, you're both sick!"*

Finally, she decided to open up a bit. She said, "I never liked Michael at all, and neither did any of my girls." Suddenly, as if I was now speaking with a completely different person, she started to deny being with him again; I was about ready to jump through the phone and shake her. So once again, I warned her about being straight with me. She said, "Why do you think that Julia's baby, Katie, belongs to Michael, instead of Jonathan?"

You know what? Wait one minute. I said, *"I am going to forgive you!"* You could have heard a pin drop as silence filled the air. I said, *"I am going to forgive you, because firstly I need to get on with my life, and secondly because I think that the two of you need psychiatric help! You definitely have some screws lose. Do you think your grandchildren would like to know how you messed up their good friend's family? I promise you, I will give them every detail if you give me any more of your fricken lies! I am going to ask you this one last time, and I want to know right now, whether or not you and Michael have been together since I found out about your repulsive affair?"*

She said, "Well, I have to tell you that he calls me all the time." I said, *"When was the last time you spoke to my husband?"* She said, "About two weeks ago, and he wanted to get back together with me."

That was enough for me, and anything that was holding my body together had come completely unglued. I knew once again that my suspicions were right, and that Michael was up to no good. I said, *"If I catch you two together ever again, I promise you, I will tell all of your grandchildren what a bitch you are, and how you helped destroy peoples' lives!"* She said, "Why are you taking this out on Julia? You two don't even talk."

I said, *"I'm not taking this out on Julia. She hasn't called me in over a year, and has a new love since Jonathan passed away. Some of our mutual friends knew about her new relationship, but for some reason she decided to keep it from me. You have been to several of our family functions while still having a sexual relationship with Michael. Therefore, you obviously have no conscience. Why don't you let me worry about Julia and myself? This is yours and Michael's fault. Do you really think her and I can go back to the friendship we once had, being like sisters, when her mother and my husband have been engaged in sexual fantasies for over a decade?"*

She said, "You two had the best friendship in the world, you shouldn't throw that away!" I thought she seriously had some screws loose! I had to put my thoughts together, and try to calm down a bit now before confronting Michael with this.

I paged him at work, and within a few minutes, he returned my call with the usual, "Hi, Hon!" I wasn't in the mood for false mushy stuff, and it took all of about twenty seconds of small talk for me to say, *"Michael, I'm going to ask you one more time whether or not you have made any contact with Martha recently?"*

His reply was, "No! Of course not! I have told you on more than one occasion that I have no reason to contact her, or be with her. I have not spoken with her in almost two years. All I want is you and the girls. Can't you see that?"

This was my cue, and the froth began to flow. I said, *"By the way, Michael, guess who I just got off the phone with?"* Of course he was clueless, and said, "Who?" I said, *"Martha!"* He said, "And?" *"And she told me that you had been in contact with her, and wanted to start up the relationship again."*

He said, "That's not true!" I said, *"You are nothing but a fucking pathological lying bastard, and I hate your guts! I should have known from the beginning that you would never change!"* Finally, he said, "Okay, I just called her to see how things were going, and to see why you and Julia were still not talking!"

There really was nothing else he could say to me, and I was livid. Michael said, "I'm sorry, it won't happen again," and by now my body felt more like ice cream in a blender, spinning out of control. I just had to hang up.

It came as no surprise the following evening that he came home with flowers; flowers grown from seeds of guilt and dishonesty. With my mind still clouded with anger, I tried to be rational, and think of what I was going to do. I couldn't leave him because without him, the girls and I had no insurance, and he held the key to all our finances.

Did I want to see him on the streets pushing a shopping cart? No, I couldn't do that to my children's father, so that must mean that perhaps I had a screw loose. Michael knew that I was raised with strong Italian family values, and that I wouldn't throw a dog into the street, and he certainly took advantage of it; but he had obviously lost sight of his family values a long time ago.

55

Any man could be a father but not necessarily a daddy. Throughout the years I had had the pleasure of getting our girls involved in many activities including swim team, dance team, modeling, tennis, gymnastics, violin, and more. I was sure that I could count on one hand how many of these activities Michael had attended or participated in.

Yes, sometimes he was working, and unable to attend or participate, but what about all the quality times he missed seeing his little girls grow up when he was off with his girlfriend? It was his loss because he had missed three beautiful little girls, and all the joy they had brought into my life. I personally enjoyed every minute with my girls, and all the activities they had been involved with throughout the years.

What about the concerts? I had become the concert Mom, and attended many concerts, and ice shows with the girls. Yes I was in there with the rest of the screaming teens enjoying Backstreet Boys, N'Sync, and several other country concerts. These were all memories I held dear to my heart. When you were sitting in an arena, and the band you came to see came out onto the stage, talk about an adrenaline rush! Oh my goodness, and my hearing? What did you say? When you see your child's eyes get as big as saucers, and their little faces light up with such excitement, you know that even though you were temporarily hearing impaired, and had no voice when you left, it was worth more than words could express.

All three of them were exceptional dancers, and were in lots of competitions when they were younger. Millie and Madison seemed to really excel in swimming, especially the "butterfly stroke," and Madeline's favorite thing in the whole world was modeling; she also loved to sing and dance.

My health still seemed to be an issue, and my doctor had recommended that I go to one of the major medical centers. My good friend, Gail, came along with me for moral support, and of course we always had a few good laughs. All of these diagnostic studies and appointments seemed to be taking forever. My goodness, one could be dead before they figured out what was wrong, or should I say whether or not the new suspicious lump you had was cancer.

Meanwhile, even though I was waiting on test results, I continued to study for my State Real Estate exam, at least two to three hours every day. I was determined to pass this test the first time, and I had lots of support from my family and friends, without whom I'm not sure how I could have done any of what I have done.

Our cabana swim season had started, and the girls were having a great time. We had lots of friends, children as well as adults that we got to mingle with on a daily basis at the pool. Most days while watching the kids swim, I would sit with a few of my other Mom friends including Gail, Maureen, Rhonda, and some others. I couldn't possibly name all of our friends, but we all shared a common bond and interest, which were our children.

Our pool family was quite a special group, and we had such a great time watching all the kids swim, while discussing our everyday lives. Most of the kids attended the same schools, and we so often had many things in common to discuss. Gail was actually an elementary school teacher, and some of our children had been fortunate enough to be in her class; she was a wonderful teacher, and friend, and two of her three children, Katie and Tim, swam on our team.

April 23rd was a very special day for us, especially for Madeline, as she turned thirteen that day. Not only was it her birthday but it also fell on Easter that year. I couldn't believe that she was already a teenager, and hadn't given me any gray hairs yet!

Our new little teenybopper was all of about five feet two inches tall, and soaking wet weighed in at around seventy-eight pounds. She looked like a little Barbie doll with her golden tan, olive-shaped brown eyes, and medium-blonde, long naturally curly hair.

Even though she was my carefree child, she still insisted that she was going to be the next "teen sensation!" She loved to sing and dance. We had her party at a fifties restaurant, and invited several of her teenybopper friends, as well as all five of my nieces.

The day after Easter and Madeline's birthday, she realized that there really wasn't an Easter Bunny, and I will take the blame for that. Even though I had put out the baskets, with having so much on my plate, hiding the eggs totally slipped my mind.

Anyway, it got the girls to thinking, which turned into a major family discussion as to whether or not the Easter Bunny was real. I asked her if she believed in him, and she said, "Yes," but clearly was not convinced, and kept insisting that I tell her.

I had always believed that when a child was ready to know about the Easter Bunny, Tooth Fairy, and Santa that you should tell them the truth. So I told her that I was the Easter Bunny, which caused her to laugh hysterically.

This was going to raise another important person or character; that of the Tooth Fairy, and this time Madison would be asking the questions. The timing was just too perfect because they had just finished watching an adorable movie called *Toothless*.

Madison said, "Mommy, if you are the Easter Bunny, does that mean that you are the Tooth Fairy too?" The expression on their faces was priceless. I said, *"Yes, I am the Tooth Fairy as well."* Madeline and Madison broke out into uncontrollable laughter. Neither of them believed me so I told them to go and ask Millie.

However, Millie was in the shower, and didn't know that I had told them that, so when they went into the bathroom to ask her, she just gave them a puzzled look, but didn't say a word. Madeline and Madison came back down the hallway and Madison said, "Mommy, please tell me, are you the Tooth Fairy or not?"

Once again, I said, *"Yes, Madison, I swear I am the Tooth Fairy!"* She then said to me, "Mommy, get a life," and ran back down the hallway to see Millie again. Meanwhile, I yelled down the hallway to Millie to tell her sisters the truth and she said, "Yes, girls, Mommy is the Tooth Fairy and I am her helper!"

Well, there we were again, with all of us laughing hysterically. I never realized telling them would be this much fun. I was sure that it wouldn't be long before they were asking about Santa Claus.

Usually by this age most kids knew the truth, however we had done such a good job, and had been so creative over the years, that the girls were able to believe and enjoy as long as possible.

April showers bring May flowers. It was May already, and life itself was in full bloom. Millie and Bryce had somewhat mended fences, and decided to at least remain good friends. Even though Bryce was a senior, Millie's Junior Prom was coming up, and just like with the Christmas Ball the two of them went together as a very handsome couple; they looked so good together, and when they looked at each other, it was just like magic.

It was another night for all of us to remember, and even though they went as just friends this time, they did in fact enjoy each other's company. Unfortunately for Millie, within a week Bryce had asked another girl to his Senior Ball, instead of her, and she was crushed. That was the last straw for her with regards Bryce.

I drove down to Sacramento to take my State Real Estate Exam by myself; it was a two-and-a-half hour drive, and I needed to stay focused on the drive, as well as remember what I had studied. With my pending medical problem, I prayed that while taking the test I was able to stay focused and not worry about it. By noon, all of us students had started our exam.

For a while I seemed to be doing fine, until I suddenly started to feel this apprehension setting in, and those nagging cancer thoughts in the back of my mind sneaking into focus. I was just about ready to say, *"I can't do this"* when the positive side of my personality kicked in, and I said to myself, *"No, I'm not stopping, I am going to pass this exam!"*

I managed to finish the exam in half the time needed; all the hard work and determination seemed to have been worth it. I was ecstatic when I turned my exam into the proctor, and left the room completely overcome with joy.

Yes! I just knew that I had passed. It would be a week before I would get official word from the State as to whether or not I did actually pass, and the news was good; I passed my State Exam, and was now a licensed Realtor. I was so pleased with what I had accomplished. After all, it had been over twenty-seven years since I had been in school. All of my family and friends that had supported all my diligent efforts were very pleased with my results.

The girls had swim team practice every afternoon, and we were all really enjoying being out at the pool with our friends. We are all very proud of our children; they were all swimming so well during practice, as well as at all the Saturday swim meets we attended. Just imagine four male teenagers, ages fifteen thru eighteen, sporting bikinis and one-piece suits over their Speedos, as well as swim caps.

Well that was exactly what our four stout young men did at one of our swim meets. Were they embarrassed? No, of course not! It was Richard, Robert, Bryan, and Patrick, all of who enjoyed the overabundance of attention they received, especially from the young ladies. They didn't just put these suits on to model them either; they got up onto the starting blocks, and dove in to swim their final relays, consuming the crowd that was overcome with laughter, and cheering, and they won the race.

With summer in full swing, the girls were enjoying being out of school, and being young ladies of leisure. I would have loved to take them on a little trip down south to Disneyland and Universal Studios again; unfortunately it all depended on what my doctors decided to do with me.

The surgeon now wanted to do another biopsy to remove abnormal lymph nodes that were present. This health issue had gone on for much too long, but fortunately for me, I had lots of support from my family and friends. Gail, Maureen, and Rhonda, were all taking turns coming with me to my appointments to help keep me sane.

There was something I had to do before going into surgery. They say the truth will set you free? How about when you need to find that tender spot in your heart and forgive someone for hurting you so terribly? I wondered if this would set me free. I was going into surgery the following week, and God forbid something should happen to me, I had lots of consequential issues I wanted to resolve that had gone unresolved.

I wondered if I could get to Heaven without forgiving Michael? Was I going to feel better about it, and be able to put the past behind me, or should I say us? I wondered what Michael would do if I were to forgive him?

56

One evening while in the middle of yet another heated discussion about our relationship, and Michael wanting us to rekindle that old flame, I decided it was time for me to forgive him. I looked straight into his emerald greens, and said, *"Michael, I forgive you."* With a vacuous stare, he said, "Yeah, right, nothing has changed since I confessed to you. That isn't forgiveness."

I said, *"Michael, I am forgiving you because I know in my heart that it is the right thing to do. You were raised a Catholic, weren't you? You know what forgiveness is, right? I have friends that have forgiven the man that took their daughter's life while driving, and being completely obliterated. I am forgiving you Michael, sincerely. This doesn't mean that I think what you did was right. What you did was completely unacceptable. However, I can't move forward with my life, our lives, and carry hatred with me every day. It's just not healthy, and it takes the burden off how I am feeling and it becomes entirely your problem, not mine. For months on end I have driven myself crazy dealing with your infidelity, but not anymore. I hope that you have learned from this, and can become a stronger person from it. It's now up to you as to how you choose to live your life."*

Waiting, waiting, and more waiting to see what all of my specialists were going to decide to do with my biopsy results. They had already told me that my body had the propensity for cancer, which was not comforting. I was headed back to the major medical center, where I was hopeful they could resolve this expeditiously. The doctors had told me that my case was extremely complex, but I was tired of being bounced back and forth.

I had undergone weeks and weeks of diagnostics. Maureen had been with me every day when I had received special nuclear injections, which followed a three-week period of no sodium, dairy products, or red food dyes, which would interfere with the accuracy of this particular full body nuclear scan.

I became very sick and lethargic with these injections, and almost felt as if I had been poisoned. This procedure and scan would ultimately give us a clear blueprint of what was going on in my body, and hopefully would conclude all the studies they had put me through.

It was Friday, the most dreaded day of the week, the day the results of the nuclear scan were in. As Maureen and I sat in the lobby area, I didn't think my chest had the capacity to hold my heart, which appeared to be pumping well beyond the realm of normal.

My doctor came into the waiting room with his associate to get me. The bleak expression on their faces was terrifying, and even without them speaking, I knew that something was wrong.

"*Oh, my gosh,*" I thought. The atmosphere in the exam room was frigid and still. The mood of the two doctors was somber, and I was convinced that if they had had any good news, they would have already shared it with me in the lobby area.

As my doctor carefully placed my films up onto the lighted screen, he proceeded to tell me, as well as show me the problem areas in my neck region. I couldn't believe what I was seeing. What was that big black spot on my windpipe? What were all of those luminous areas surrounding it?

Batting away my tears, I had to try to stay focused on what he was telling me. Even though he was speaking, I couldn't really hear him. I could see his lips moving as if in slow motion, without sound. The only thing I knew at that moment was "cancer."

Even though I was awake, I suddenly felt a bit comatose. The only good news was that it appeared to be localized in my neck area, not attacking the rest of my body, thank goodness. But what was I going to tell my girls? Hadn't we endured enough?

Some of my friends said this was a test of my faith, and I said, *"Dear Lord, if this is a test, how much more do you want to put on my plate? I no longer have a plate but more like a platter you have filled for me. I don't understand why some people's faith in you is tested, and why you don't give equal portions to everyone?"*

My doctor had explained to me that he couldn't force me to do anything but recommended radiation treatment. Before they could do that, I would have to endure another three weeks of the special diet and injections.

My exam was over, and I felt as if I was in a fog. I walked out into the lobby where Maureen was waiting for me. I had blocked out the entire world, with the exception of what I had just seen and heard. My legs were moving, and I could hear my footsteps, but it was as if someone was moving them for me.

Maureen could tell from my gloomy appearance that our deepest fears had been realized; she had an overwhelming amount of love and support for me, and I don't think I could have gone that far without her by my side.

We drove around for a couple of hours just talking, and trying to help me figure out life, and why it had so many detours before you could get to where you wanted to go. We went back to the house where all of our kids, Millie, Madeline, Madison, Kathleen, and Bobby, had just had a pizza delivered, and were having a great time together as usual.

Throughout all of this, I had had lots of love and support from everyone; I knew beyond any doubt that my family and friends were always there for me. My parents were retired by then, and had enough of their own problems without having to deal with mine. How could I dump this on them again?

Just because they were my parents, didn't mean they should always be the dumpees. My brother, Tony, and sister-in-law, Maria, had always been there for my girls, and me too, in many immeasurable ways. They had given me five beautiful nieces, now ranging in ages from two to twelve years old.

I adored them, and cherished the times we spent together. When we got all our girls together, their five and our three, you had eight of the happiest kids around. It always made us very proud of them to see how much they loved and respected one another.

Another very important person in my life was my friend, Honey. She was the principal at my girls' Elementary school for many years, and we had kept an ongoing friendship. I can remember back when every Wednesday morning, I would go to our favorite coffee shop and pick up three lattes for her and I, and one for our other friend, the secretary of our school, Glenda.

I remember her telling all the students one year that if they reached their goals for a particular function the school was sponsoring, she would roller-skate around for one full day dressed up as a clown. Well she kept her word, and she made the most adorable and colorful principal I think anyone ever could have. I personally had an enormous amount of respect for her. She was truly an inspiration to me, and carried the wisdom of the world.

I never had any regrets about my girls' education under her supervision at their Elementary school. We were most fortunate to have had an abundance of wonderful teachers on the staff as well. Whether it was Ms. Sharon, Millie, Carol, Joyce, Kathy, Gail, Carolyn, Sherri, or Mr. Bryan, my girls received a strong educational foundation from all of them.

The years there weren't uneventful by any means, but something that I will always treasure. During all my years of volunteering at the school, I met and became friends with lots of people including, Mary M., Elaine S., Gail O., Jeannie G., to name a few. Honey was in charge of all of us, and it was a pleasure to work with all of them.

57

Well my girls were not yet aware that I was going to have to endure radiation treatment. It had been my belief all along to let them have as normal a childhood as possible, and give them little, if anything, to worry about, unless it was absolutely necessary. This particular scenario did warrant me discussing it with them in detail, but with caution. How did you find the right words to tell your children you were going to need radiation? I didn't think there were any proper words for that situation. It would not be easy for me, nor would it be easy for them to hear.

My girls were all frightened beyond their own comprehension; there were tears and many questions. If I could have read their minds, I would have to say they were thinking their Mommy was going to die of cancer. I could just feel it in my heart, and even though I didn't convey it to them, deep down I had my own fears and doubts about the treatments, and their effectiveness in treating the cancer.

I had always kept extremely busy with my girls, and enjoyed every moment that I was with them. It also helped to take my mind off the things that I really didn't want to deal with, and had a way of putting life into a better perspective.

Michael's response to all of this came as no surprise whatsoever; it was almost as if I were inviting him out for coffee. All he said was, "I think it's time the two of us spent some quality time together." What was he thinking? We hadn't spent quality time together in such a long time, and suddenly he wanted to spend time with me? Was he afraid I was going to die now?

My good friend, Gail, was back in town. She had been on vacation for almost three weeks, and I had really missed her. She had been a wonderful friend, and I would always cherish our friendship. In fact, Madison would be staying with her and her family for a few days while I was in the hospital. Her and Katie would have a great time playing together.

Millie and Madeline wanted to stay with Grandma and Grandpa, where they would also be able to spend time with my nieces; Felicia, Livia, Maria, Petrina, and Cristina. I knew they were all going to be well taken care of, but I was still going to miss them very much.

I had nowhere to run, and nowhere to hide; it was the gloomy day on which I was being admitted to the hospital for treatments.

Michael had to work, which was fine. Gail and Maureen volunteered to pick me up, and bring me to the medical center. Rhonda was on vacation, or I know she would have wanted to come along too.

Gail and Maureen showed up at my house to take me to the medical center, and I reluctantly grabbed my bags and we all headed for Gail's van. It was really somewhat funny because Maureen thought I had gone over the edge, and feared me jumping out of the van. I promised her that I wouldn't though.

Besides, I knew she would chase me with a whiffle bat. She and I had this small joke between us, which would always give us a good laugh. Whenever I didn't want to do something I was supposed to, she would always say, "I'm going to get the bat out!" She was a very kind person, and would never really do anything like this, but it certainly made us laugh each time she said it.

While Gail was driving, and Maureen was navigating, I tried to give Gail the wrong exit in the hopes she would miss the one we needed, and I wouldn't have to go. No such luck, they didn't want to listen to my directions, and knew exactly what I was doing.

With the sun shining so brightly, it was really quite warm out that day. As we drove up the highway with the beautiful deep green, rolling hills on both sides, I could see a blanket of cattle and horses covering the countryside. Momentarily, I got lost in my thoughts. The closer we got to the medical center, the sicker my body felt and the more my eyes began to well up. Gail had this goodie bag she had put together for me to use during my stay in the hospital.

Third floor, Nurses station, "Can we help you?"
"Hi, I'm Sara Tenaci, and I was just admitted for radiation treatment. I'm supposed to be put into an isolation ward."

The nurse brought me to my room, which didn't appear to look anything like an isolated area. The view from my room overlooked the garden, but nonetheless was still a very gloomy room. The preparations for my room were not complete yet, so when their special nuclear team showed up, we would have to leave for about an hour.

"My name is____?" Well, even though she was very pleasant, I don't remember her name. When the nurse came into my room and asked which one of us was Sara, I pointed to Gail. The three of us burst into laughter, and soon the nurse figured out that it was I that weighed in at about one hundred and one pounds. I wasn't quite ready to get into the bed so the three of us just stood next to the windowsill like the "Three Musketeers."

I tried my best to make light of the situation, along with Gail and Maureen. All of us were very observant as to what was going on in my room. After all, they were feeling my apprehension as well. The bed sheets didn't live up to our expectations and scrutiny; the first set had a couple of hairs on them, so we had them changed.

The second set had holes in them so we had them changed again. I guess our indirect intention was to make them as miserable as they were about to make me. Not really, but it was somewhat funny.

Eventually the nuclear team showed up clad in their puke-green duds, and we were asked to leave the room for a while. However, just before we walked out, we all broke into hysterical laughter once again; the third set of sheets had been put on with the utmost perfection, and the nuclear tech came in and ripped them all the way back for his preparation of this morgue-like setting.

While walking down the hall in an attempt to find some serenity, my doctors decided they wanted to meet with me in a conference room for a few moments, and go over some of the treatment protocol. Gail and Maureen weren't allowed in, so they decided to wander the halls for a while. My doctor told me he was going to give me a much higher dose of the internal radiation than expected, in the hopes it would work, and wouldn't have to be repeated.

This was becoming very depressing. When we were finished with the discussion, I went out into the hallway as if in a daze in the hopes of finding my friends. I couldn't find them anywhere, and became quite nervous. My eyes were once again welling up, and the tears were rolling down my cheeks. If they didn't show up soon, I was going to call a cab and leave!

Finally, they came walking around the corner by the lounge. Boy, was I ever happy to see them, instead of someone in medical attire. Soon another one of my doctors showed up to escort us to my room. I didn't have a calm bone in my body, and if I could have, I would have bolted right out of there.

She said, "You look nervous and scared, don't be nervous, it's not going to be bad." Well, I knew that she was trying to comfort me, but it wasn't going to work. After arriving at the door to my puke-green isolation unit, she asked my friends to wait outside so that she could take my vitals and such.

I entered the room, and felt as if I were going into a spaceship prepared for some sick alien from the outer limits. But I had the most wonderful surprise on my window sill, which I will never forget, because just when I was feeling so completely melancholy, Gail and Maureen had come into my room and fixed up the windowsill with all my little packages, and two brightly-colored bouquets, accompanied by teddy bears and cards. It was a very pleasant surprise, and certainly did help lift my spirits. It sure did help light up my dismal looking domicile.

As I looked around, I took notice of the two huge nuclear waste boxes for disposing of anything and everything that I would come into contact with. They were wrapped in pea-green plastic, and sealed with tape. Even my phone had nuclear protection on it. The floors, knobs, items fastened down or not were completely covered with this pea green paper, and tape. Even the floors in my room and bathroom were covered and taped down. Well, with the exception of the shower, which looked halfway decent.

Finally, yet importantly, the good old Nuclear Med danger signs on the outside of my door telling everyone to "Stay Out!" That's right, I was not going to be allowed any visitors, and the hospital personnel could only come into my habitat for a very limited amount of time, so that they weren't overly exposed to the radiation.

As I waited with an intense amount of anxiety for my doctors to allow Gail and Maureen back in, I think I wore out the protective coverings on the floor by pacing back and forth. Finally, they were allowed back in, and we had a few more minutes to chat while waiting for "Dr. Doom" to arrive with the nuclear meds cart.

Dr. Doom arrived, and totally freaked me out. He spoke briefly to all of us, and then told them to get their hugs in before leaving. They would have to be out of there before he could administer the radiation. He also told them that if anyone saw me wandering the halls after treatment had started that they would "Shoot on sight!" Of course he was joking, but we all got the picture.

Gail and Maureen had left, and my doctor had told them to look up at my window over the garden when leaving, and they would be able to see me. So we waited a couple of minutes, and I walked over to the window to wave goodbye to them. It was now going to be just "me, myself and I." How depressing.

I was given my mega dose of internal radiation in the hopes that it would be more effective than the beam radiation. This would work more like chemotherapy because it was systemic, and would travel throughout my entire body, including my vascular and lymph systems. I was given anti-nausea meds to help me tolerate the radiation, and was left with very specific instructions on what to do and not do, at which time the doctors left my isolation area.

58

By this time, I had opened up my surprise packages from Gail, which included crayons, drawing paper, crossword puzzles, playing cards, and a magazine, obviously designed to keep me more than occupied. After my tummy settled a bit with the anti-nausea meds, they brought me a restricted diet meal, including pale orange diced carrots, fluffy white rice, and something that resembled the sole of my shoe, which I think was supposed to be pork, but none of which had any salt or seasonings.

Staying there was quite depressing especially because I missed my three girls. In between being sick and feeling lonely, I either tried to keep myself busy with the books Maureen brought, or all the other supplies Gail gave me. There was plenty to occupy me, but nothing could hold my interest.

All I kept thinking was that I had this radiation running through my veins trying to ferret out the cancer cells and atomize them, while at the same time really frightening me.

In the wee hours of the morning, a male nurse came in to give me an anti-nausea injection in my buttocks, which supposedly gave the quickest relief; so much for modesty.

Eventually I was able to fall asleep, only to be awakened by an earsplitting scream. I had double doors into my room because of the isolation rules, and the nurse stood in between the two of them at five-thirty in the morning yelling, "Did you pee?"

I thought I was hearing things and said, *"Excuse me?"* She said, "Did you pee?" I thought that was what she had said, but how rude! I said, *"No, I didn't pee! My goodness, I'm trying to sleep, would you like me to pee?"* She said, "Yes."

So... there I was in the wee hours of the morning going to pee for her, so that she could run her lab work. Even though I was beyond fatigued, I figured that I might as well just take my shower.

Initially I would only have to stay in the hospital until the second day. However, I would be released with quite a few restrictions, so that I didn't overexpose anyone to the radiation that would remain in my system for some time.

I couldn't have my kids around me for the first week, and then for a while after that they would have to remain several feet away to reduce the radiation exposure. This would be the most difficult thing for me to do because I loved my girls more than life itself. Not being allowed to cuddle with them, or give them hugs and kisses for a while was going to be arduous. Nevertheless, if that was what I had to do to keep them safe from harm, it was worth it.

I called Michael at work to come pick me up, and bring me home. It must have been a sweltering one hundred and five degrees out that day, and he came in his car with no air conditioning; and wouldn't you just know it? The car started to overheat on the highway. I thought I might have to call a cab in my jammies.

We argued all the way home, because Michael didn't even call me while I was in the hospital. He really took advantage of the fact that I couldn't check up on his whereabouts; his excuse was that he didn't know what hospital I was admitted to. What a crock that was! Whatever, it was more important for me to get healthy so that I could take care of my girls.

Once again, I started to think about Michael, the man I fell in love with and married. I didn't know what had come over him the past twenty years. He had so many extraordinary qualities, but somehow always managed to let the negative qualities dominate them.

I thought to myself that this man, Michael, was kind and would do anything for our girls and me. So, why did he insist on living a double life? What was it he was trying to prove to himself in this lifetime? He had a family that loved him very much, and would do anything for him, so why did it seem like he was still searching? Over the course of our marriage, I had tried many times to figure it out, but was still completely puzzled.

I looked back on Michael's family life, how it was for him before we met, and wondered. Actually, I more than wondered what kind of an impact his childhood had had on his adult life. I think it had a great deal to do with the man that he was, and his behavior. I believed in my heart that in many ways Michael was alone, and searching for himself. I didn't know anyone who could help him discover, and bring to light who he really was. Sometimes finding oneself could be an endless journey through life.

A couple of weeks had passed since the radiation, and life seemed to be moving along beautifully. The kids were back in school, and we had all resumed our normal schedule. Millie was already a senior in high school, and would be graduating that year. Many of her good friends had graduated the previous year, so she wasn't too happy. However, she still had her good friends Kristen, Tania, Amy, Ashleigh, and Rachel, to name a few.

Madeline was in seventh grade, and had become a real social butterfly. It was cute to watch her bubbly personality when she was with good friends such as, Jenna S., Katie I., or Kathleen M. Jenna and Madeline had been good friends since they had baby teeth.

Madison was in sixth grade, and was just a bit apprehensive with this being her first year in middle school. I was not too worried though; she had always had an outgoing personality, and got along with almost everyone. She too had many special friends that she had grown up with since kindergarten. One of which was Renae, who was also on her swim team. The girls seemed to have adjusted quite well to the new school year, as well as enjoying being with all of their old friends. When the kids were happy, Mom was happy.

It was hard to believe that I had another adult in my house now; Millie had just turned eighteen years old, although it seemed like just yesterday that I gave that all so special first birthday party to my adorable little girl, with the big brown eyes, and a face as round as an apple pie.

I was so proud of the young lady she had grown into. We celebrated her birthday at her favorite Mexican restaurant with several of our friends, but I knew in my heart that if Bryce had shown up she would have had a better time.

Just when I thought I had my life under control, something else was placed onto my plate; my doctors never told me that the radiation was going to cause me to lose my taste buds. Although this was supposed to be temporary, I couldn't taste anything at all.

In addition to this, I got a bloody nose every day. Why were doctors so evasive? They should have at least warned me. Now that I could eat normal, non-restricted foods, I couldn't taste them!

My family and friends gave me lots of love and support; I couldn't possibly have asked for more. They had been there for me through it all. Although I preferred denying it, I now conceded to having been treated for cancer once again. I didn't think that I would ever come to terms with it though.

I sometimes wonder about what my family and friends were thinking. When they looked at me, what was it that they really saw? Did they see me, Sara? On the other hand, did they see the cancer? Were they thinking, "Is she going to be okay, or is she going to die?" I couldn't help but wonder what went through all of their heads, because deep down when I looked at myself in the mirror, I too wondered how long it would be before the cancer came back again, and consumed my body.

Everyone often wonders how I was able to deal with all of this stress, but I can't honestly answer that because I don't really know. I just did the best that I could, and tried to be positive about the outcome.

Having to deal with several life-threatening illnesses over the years did ominous things to my self-esteem. I didn't think it was asking too much to want a normal life. When I look in the mirror, I see a woman standing before me whose body and mind has been through hell, but you would have to walk a mile in my shoes to know.

59

Well, there was still one more biopsy yet to be determined on my neck. The pathologist had found some transforming cells. It was very likely that these were malignant, but not related to the same cancer type that I had already been treated for.

So what did this mean? Did I have a secondary cancer? Unfortunately, I had continued to have problems with my salivary glands. However, with everything that I had already been through I had agreed with my doctor that the only way I was having surgery again was if the nodules actually became larger. Besides, it hadn't even been long enough yet for the radiation to completely ablate the other cancer cells.

A blast from the past had been speaking to me online, and would also have liked to speak with Millie again. Yes, it was Bryce, the young man that had broken my daughter's heart. From time to time in the past, I had had many deep conversations with him online with regard to their relationship.

I wasn't happy that Millie had her heart broken, but that wasn't any reason for me to dislike him. They were young, and things like that happened. He was still a very respectful young man.

On several occasions, he confided in me his true feelings for Millie. He was always good to her. When he broke up with her, he thought he was doing the right thing. Their relationship had grown so intense, and at such a rapid pace that his feelings frightened him a bit.

The conversation I remembered most with him was when he told me that, "Millie came into his life much too soon." He explained to me that Millie was the kind of girl he wanted to marry when the time was right. There would be several years between then and four years of college. Who knew what the two of them would be doing when that time came?

Anyway, to get back to the online instant messaging with him, he seemed to be very interested in how Millie was doing, and what she was up to. He wanted to wish her a belated eighteenth birthday.

For several nights, he would be online, and tell me to say "hi" to Millie for him. The reason he was so apprehensive about doing it himself was because after Millie found out that he was taking someone else to his Senior Ball the two of them had a major falling out, and really hadn't spoken since. She just figured that with another girl in his life, their relationship and friendship was over, and even though it was difficult, had made up her mind to move forward with her life without him.

Within a few days, he set all his apprehensions aside, and asked to speak to Millie online. Millie tried desperately to pretend that she wasn't interested, but I could see that glimmer in her eyes, and that smile she had suppressed for so long was now enveloping her pretty face.

It was unbelievable, and I knew at that moment, that deep down she still had a fire burning for him in her heart. The two of them seemed to have set aside the anger, and were going to try to rebuild the friendship they once had.

By the end of the week they were actually speaking not only online, but via the phone as well. He was living in Santa Monica then, so it was a little difficult to just drop in for a cup of coffee. Bryce asked Millie what she would do if he suddenly showed up at her door, and she told him that we would probably have to call 911.

Bryce and I had always been good at keeping surprises from Millie, and that time was no exception. The plan was to tell her that he was having a package delivered for her, and that he would call her when the courier notified him that he was outside of our apartment so that she could go outside to accept it.

Millie had absolutely no idea, but Bryce and I knew that he was the package that would be arriving that weekend. Millie was not only thrilled that the two of them were speaking again, but overcome with joy that he was sending her something.

She was going bananas trying to figure out what the package was. Our plan worked like a charm; he called her from his cell phone and pretended that he was en route to San Diego to see his cousin, when in fact he was en route to see her.

During this time, he continued to talk to her on the phone for well over an hour, and then said that he would call her back as soon as he heard from the courier. I had to pretend that nothing was happening, although I was the only one that knew what was going on. We didn't tell Madeline or Madison because we thought maybe they would get excited, and spill the beans.

Millie's phone rang, and it was Bryce calling. There was that beautiful smile again and she said, "It's Bryce, and he said that my package is here!" So I played dumb and watched as she opened the front door. I followed right behind her to see what this package was, knowing the whole time exactly what it was going to be. As she went out onto the balcony, she didn't really know what to expect. Suddenly she turned to look toward the front of our complex, and there he was.

She could see him there with this beautiful smile, holding out his arms with his cell phone in one of them talking to her. I thought I was going to have to blow in her face to get her to breathe. I said, *"There's your surprise package!"*

What a moment that was, and it made the hairs on my arms stand up. It was like a scene from Pretty Woman. It took a few seconds for her to realize that it was in fact Bryce standing there, and suddenly she screamed, "Oh, my goodness!" and went running down the stairs, as the two of them ran toward each other. He picked her up, took her in his arms, and twirled her around. It was like magic all over again. I could say one thing; the boy definitely had charisma.

We were well into October, and the two of them seemed to have rekindled their friendship. In fact, he had helped her out at my niece's school, where she was coaching volleyball. The kids all got a kick out of it when he showed up to help. When he spiked the ball, it wasn't like anything they had ever seen. I knew that the two of them were a perfect match, and made an adorable couple.

However, whether or not they become a couple was not important; all I knew was that it was such a pleasure to see how happy Millie was with Bryce coming back into her life.

I hoped that she didn't get hurt again, and I just wanted the two of them to enjoy their friendship. All good relationships are built on strong friendships, and it was not up to me to decide whether the two of them should be together again. It was their decision and if it was meant for them to be together, then they would be.

The holidays were just around the corner, and I had known for a while that it wouldn't be long before Madeline and Madison started to question Santa Claus, and just how he came down the chimney, when in fact we didn't even have a fireplace. I used to always tell them that Santa had magical stardust, which worked really well until recently. This morning I was sitting there looking at some Christmas cards in a catalog, and Madeline said, "Mommy, is there really a Santa Claus?"

I don't know if it was sleep deprivation, or because it was just so darn cute, but I started to laugh; it just struck me as being so funny. I was not expecting this at seven in the morning. She got this big smile on her face and said, "Every time I talk about Santa Claus to Kathleen, she laughs!" So I said, *"Do you believe in Santa?"* Madeline looked at me with a big bright smile, and said, "Well, not if he isn't real!" So... I started to tell her about St. Nicholas and I said, *"Do you believe in the Magic of Christmas?"*

She said, "Yes, but..." Then there was the big question and she said, "Mommy, are you Santa Claus, and is Millie your helper?" We both broke out into hysterical laughter, and it was just adorable. She said, "Mommy, if you are Santa then who did we hear on the roof last Christmas?"

I said, *"That, my dear, was your father running on the roof with a big HO, HO, HO!"* Then she said,

"What about the reindeer and the bells?" I said, *"That was your father ringing the jingle bells."* Oh my goodness, it was a priceless moment, and Madeline thought this was the funniest thing she had ever heard.

Well there was still one more question, and she seemed completely confused about it. She said, "Well, if you are Santa, Millie is your helper, and Daddy was on the roof, who was that I saw standing at the Christmas tree putting presents under it last year that looked like Santa?" I said, *"That would be Grandpa!"* I thought she was going to die laughing. I told her that Grandpa would dress up every Christmas as Santa, and come over to our house and Uncle Tony's house.

Then after you were all asleep, we would wake you up a bit, and carry you one by one down the hall and say, *"Shh, look it's Santa!"* This was one of the most precious moments for us, and another beautiful memory.

Madison happened to walk into the kitchen while Madeline and I were finishing our conversation, and thought that we were making fun of Santa Claus. She wasn't happy about this, and I wasn't so sure now would be the right time to tell her that I was Santa Claus.

My sense was that she wasn't ready to know, or that she still wanted to believe in him. When she was ready, I would tell her. I didn't think she would find it as funny as Madeline had, and would be rather disappointed.

Over the years, Michael and I had made every effort to make sure the girls believed in the magic of Christmas, as well as Santa Claus. I could remember back a few years earlier when Michael and I, that would be Mr. and Mrs. Claus, would roll into action on our sleigh. That particular year Grandpa wasn't feeling well, and didn't make it over. However, Michael and I had our own plan; when we knew the girls were all asleep, I gave Michael our jumbo jingle bells, and he went out into the side yard and climbed up onto our roof.

It was nearly one in the morning, and Michael was trying to run cautiously on the roof saying, "Ho, Ho, Ho, Merry Christmas!" In addition, he rang his jingle bells. Considering I was the only one in the house awake, trying to keep my laughter as quiet as possible, I started to wake the girls up one by one.

Firstly, I went into Millie's room and said, *"Millie, listen! It's Santa, he's on the roof!"* She opened her big, brown eyes, and when she heard the thumping on the roof, the look on her face was priceless. Of course we wanted her to believe it was the reindeer. She just lay there without saying a word. It was as if she was thinking that perhaps this was just a dream. If she ever had doubts about Santa, at that moment her doubts seemed to have vanished.

Next, I went into Madeline and Madison's room. Even though the two of them were sound asleep, when I woke them their big, brown eyes just lit up like magic. I said, *"Santa's on the roof with his reindeer!"* Madison was a little bit frightened, and wasn't sure what to think. Madeline was ready to go look on the roof, but I had them both lie back down, and told them to lie there quietly and listen.

Meanwhile, Santa was running back and forth on the roof and I was thinking, *"Oh, my goodness, I hope he is careful."* Thump, thump, yes it was Michael. He had tripped on the cable wire, and fallen down on the roof.

I figured by now that we had done a good job of convincing the girls that Santa was on our roof with his reindeer, and that it was now time for him to come down. I went out into the side yard, and started to call him.

I said, *"Santa, you can come down now!"* The entire time I was laughing hysterically, and thinking to myself, what would the neighbors be thinking when they looked out their bedroom window in the wee hours of the morning, and saw me telling Santa that he could come down off the roof now?

Santa must have been way at the other end of our house because I had to call him three of four times before he heard me. It was moments and memories like these that made everything so wonderful, and truly were a part of believing in "The Magic of Christmas."

60

As if looking deep into the ocean, it was there I would see the reflection of my life, and the many memories in my heart that I would cherish forever. Not all the memories were happy ones, but they were still memories.

There are lessons to be learned from both the propitious, as well as the adverse elements in our lives. Life is very much like a puzzle; when you have all the right pieces, everything seems to fall into place. Nonetheless if you lose or damage just one small piece, it will never be the same again.

I live by high morals and put an immense value on life, and I am teaching my children to do the same. Life is precious and should be treated with respect, and although we have been faced with an abundance of adversity, we have still managed to live a pretty normal lifestyle. I refuse to give in to any adversity, and don't believe it would be setting a good example for my children to do so.

Through it all, our girls are growing into beautiful, well-balanced, fun loving young ladies. Millie is eighteen, Madeline is thirteen, and Madison is now eleven. One might ask, "Hasn't any of this had an impact on their lives?" Yes, it certainly has, and I think they will become stronger from it. I am raising them to believe that no matter how difficult the path, you must just never give up. They have already faced so much during their childhood, and now have come to appreciate the things that most people that don't face any adversity take for granted.

Our girls know that they might wake up one morning to find all that they have is gone, so they must never take anything in life for granted.

In life we have all heard that everyone has a cross to bear, or something on their plate, so to speak. I know from experience what this is like. What can I do about it? I will continue to bring our girls up with lots of love, and be the best Mom possible. I wasn't blessed with a healthy body, but I was blessed to have three wonderful daughters who make my life complete.

I think about all the remarkable people that have crossed my path in my life, and the lives of our children. Whether they be family members or friends, they have all contributed in some way to our lives, and made them what they are today.

What about Michael? Had it all been worthwhile being married to him? Out of love, Michael and I had created three beautiful, healthy little girls, and I wouldn't change that for anything in the world. When I take a stroll down the memory lane of our very rocky marriage, I try to remember the good times, and be thankful for what I have, instead of what I don't have. I guess in some ways, things could have been much worse.

Of course I remember all the adversity, and all those things that tend to tear families apart, such as infidelity. However, I do have many cherished memories of wonderful things that have taken place in our lives, which definitely made my life worth living.

I don't know if Michael and I will ever be able to rekindle the fire the two of us once shared as husband and wife; I only know that forgiving him was in fact the right thing to do. I try not to worry about the things that I can't change, and concentrate all my efforts into the things that I can make a difference with in our lives, and the lives of our children.

We have what's called "A Circle Of Life." There have been many stops in the formation of the "Circle Of Life" for me, and my family, and I guess in a peculiar kind of way, that is what it's all about. There will always be something in our lives to have to deal with, some of it good, and others not so good. You might be able to just sit for hours with a good friend, enjoying a cup of coffee and discussing your lives, and then just when you think you have said and heard it all, and the coffee is gone, you come to realize that there is more, much more, but "That's Another Cup of Coffee."

You find yourself sharing yet one more thing that will in fact take another cup to explain. It seems like in my life, I have had many of those cups of coffee, and I'm sure that there is always going to be another cup. Much like the "Circle Of Life," you just keep pouring that coffee, and life just continues to move forward until complete.

ISBN 1553958889-6

9 781553 958895